When Now Becomes Too Late

The Rapture In Brief

By

TL Farley

TL Farley

Matt 11:30

xulon PRESS

12-10-10

This work is dedicated to my loving, faithful wife,
friend and editor:

Karen Ann Farley

Table of Contents

Prologue

All The Time In The World

Anumber of years ago, in Mesquite, Texas, my son, Daniel, then about three years old, seeing I was deeply troubled, came to my side, and drawing me gently down to his eye-level, peered compassionately into my soul and queried, "Dad, are you running out of time?" His question prompted an unintentional but spontaneous explosion of memories all related to time.

One morning, years behind that moment, I was teaching a Sunday school class of fourth grade boys and girls in San Antonio, TX. Wishing to redeem the time, and not seeing a clock around, I challenged the children with, "Who has a watch?"

Gleeful giggles and laughs tumbled out as they each scrambled to bring out his or her individual timepiece. One had a Mickey Mouse, unaware of the capturing of fashion, another an old grandfather's pocket watch with big face and plain numbers. More were of the latest digital sports model variety. A young voice chimed in, "I've got micro seconds!" "We won't need that!" I impatiently intoned, embarrassingly reminded of the crush of the hour. Immediate consideration forced me to qualify my correction, "But, hang onto it, we may need it."

A backward reel of the wheel and the years fell away to a winter morning in northern Illinois with a black sky studded with stars and a distant silver moon no bigger than a dime and another little boy hurrying, late for his altar boy duties at early weekday Mass.

Cold flecks of snow brush his face as he hunches his head down deeper into his winter coat. Hands jammed into his pockets, crunching through the ice-mantled snow, walking, running and trotting, he scurries through the pre-dawn late winter hastening to be on time for God.

He frowns as he breaks through a sheet of ice and into a hidden puddle. Shaking his shoe loose of the water he races on. The Father will not excuse tardiness and it will never do to have word get out that lateness is a habit of this one, especially where God is concerned. The boy's seeming lack of attention to punctuality is already a matter of concern to a number of the Sisters, and most would be surprised to discover his heart's desire is to honor and serve the Lord with his life. Being allowed to be an altar boy is merely the first rung on a ladder he dreams to climb in God's service. And it's the first day of the workweek, Monday morning, the worst time of all to be late.

Clouds of steam billowing from his mouth and nostrils, the boy comes into view of the church, a block away. All is dark, even across the way at the convent. He must be early. Wonderful. Early is fine, even better still. He pushes on the last bit of the way.

Coming astride the massive old sanctuary, he climbs through the mounds of accumulated snow pushed back off the sidewalks, and heads down the dark passage between the Rectory and the Church. If he were not on appointment to meet with God he would be terrified. But he is, so all is well. And of course, the priest will be there. He's always early.

Finally, the lad is at the steps and climbing up to the tiny vestibule at the back. The screened outer door creaks open, as he pushes old snow back, and the boy then turns the handle to the inner door of the Sacristy.

But it's locked. He can't believe it. He tries again. Panting more quietly now, his straining abating, he grows still and listens in the dark. There is no sound but the faint drip, dripping of the icicles hanging down off the roof eaves. Retreating out and back down the steps he turns to the Rectory. All is silent and dark as a tomb. In fact, there are no sounds or signs of life anywhere. It is as if all human life has vanished.

He stumbles back down the long passage between the buildings, struggling to understand. Memories of ancient prophecies begin to creep into his mind. "Heaven and earth shall pass away, but My words will by no means pass away." (Matthew 24:35) [1]

And something about Jesus coming back and taking all believers out of the world begins to materialize in the distant recesses of his consciousness. Surely this couldn't be the time? He believed in Jesus. He tried to confess all of his sins to the priests. He hadn't forgotten any, had he?

Stumbling out into the dim light of the street lamps, he gapes about him. The day seems colder instead of warmer. Surely morning cannot be far away.

The Sisters' convent is dark. No light. No sound. No traffic in the roads. Just a gentle flicker of the snow as it stings in bits, blown around by the gusts of wind.

And in the silence he begins to notice the creaking of the trees. Leafless and dead, they groan eerily, scant whistles of ancient calls untimely in their boughs.

He turns and rushes off back down the cold, dark, wet, icy streets, filled with half frozen slush, racing for home. That was the last place he'd seen life.

Into the alley beside the BP station, through the Ag complex, behind the Farm Bureau offices, across the barren lot, across the street to the Purina feed store and down the alley running along it's side and then a right turn behind the casket company he runs. Out into the alley beside the railroad warehouse and then along and over the street and across the tracks and up Nehring's factory hill, he moves as fast as his breath and stealth will enable in this frozen nocturnal world.

Bursting in the front door of home he is met with the smell of oatmeal! Someone is moving about in the kitchen. Sounds are drifting down the stairs from above. Others are waking up and getting out of bed and he is not alone! Jesus hasn't come back and left him.

His brothers and sisters, his mom, they all wonder at his early return from Mass. He'd set the alarm too early in his excitement the night before. He'd gone off to Mass much too early. None had even been up yet. He'd get a few questions at school later in the morning, for sure. Word would get out that he wasn't able to keep a schedule at all.

Yet he'd seen something that morning. A prophecy that went unheeded by most. Jesus *will* return for His Church. It not only could be possible, but it *will* happen. He'd seen the foreshadowing. And when Jesus comes for His flock, He will take them out of this world right then. And this world, as we know it, will be changed forever. A starkness magnified by the cold, empty darkness of a lonely early winter morning. All earnestness for change from that point would be amplified. That 'now' would be almost too late.

But for now, there was time. Time to grow up. Time to finish school. Time to go out into the world. There was still time. And there was still time for 'now.'

Hugging Daniel to me, I smiled in wonder as I flooded back into the present. "No, son," I whispered in his ear as I held him tightly, " We've got all the time in the world!"

CHAPTER 1

Imminent: Closer Than Soon

F inding a relevant, contemporary usage of the word 'imminent' in its' proper context becomes surprisingly easy by perusing the newspapers of the day. In an article on the mounting tensions between China and Taiwan and the possible military showdown between the two countries, the Chicago Tribune[2] printed a story in its' March 21, 2001, issue. A factor in determining the importance of the story's employment of the term is made inherently obvious by the clarifying statement, "No one suggests that conflict is imminent." Notably, the reference is to the use of nuclear missiles and their incumbent devastation.

Not imminent. No impending major catastrophe. War will not break upon the world at any moment. Yet Scripture describes an event now referred to by biblical futurists as the Rapture, that is both prophesied and proclaimed as 'imminent.' And that means at any moment starting from the 'now' of proclamation.

Of course the incorrect usage of the word is also handily obtainable, especially in the world of advertising. An immediate example would be Publishers Clearing House announcements that have in recent months, (spring, '01), been hawking Imminent Prize Awards declarations and then including the guaranteed date for the awarding of the prize. That inclusion of date eliminates the qualification of 'imminent' projection.

In his routine, a comedian once observed he didn't want to be first, he just wanted to be next. He figured that trying to get to first place wasn't worth the trials. Being next on the other hand is always considered an enviable position. If we recognize that there is time for now we also realize, spontaneously, that there is a 'next' or future. Future then begins to have its' own structure. Near future is followed by that which is further into the future, which is before those things that are in the distant future. And as the present gobbles up the near future we then begin to understand that those events that have not yet arrived, which are in the near future and moving closer are coming into the category of that which is next or imminent. Particularly, whatever is going to happen at any moment now is said to be that which is 'imminent.' But how soon is 'imminent?'

The doctrine of the Rapture includes as its' cornerstone the feature of immediacy. But before we get into the imminent aspect of the Rapture we should begin by looking at the event itself. And rightly we should first focus on the understandings, those that are found in the Body of Messiah, a.k.a. the Body of Christ. The Bible has only one teaching on the Rapture. But, of course, within the Body of Christ, the Church, there are many interpretations concerning our Blessed Hope.

Surprisingly many, if not most, Christians, at least professing Christians, do not believe in the Rapture at all. In his book, *"Every Prophecy of the Bible,"* the late Dr. John F. Walvoord, former Chancellor of Dallas Theological Seminary observed, "Though amillennialism continues to be the majority view of the Church, among those who hold a high view of Scripture the pre-millennial interpretation has been given detailed exposition, serving to provide an intelligent view of the present and the future from the standpoint of biblical prophecy."[3] Obviously, Dr. Walvoord himself was absent from that list of subscribers in the majority position, having been a theologian whose view was in agreement with those of us throughout the Body of Messiah, who listen and watch for His ordained shout and trumpet call out of this present world.

However, the bulk of Christians hold fast to the amillenial position, which is also suggested by a June 25, 2001 article in the weekly *Baptist Standard*,[4] a Dallas, TX, publication. Pumping a review that slants against the popular *Left Behind* series' collaborators, Dr. Tim LaHaye and Jerry B. Jenkins, a plug for the news story topped the front page by finishing off the series title with a question mark. The blurb read, "The best-selling Left Behind series is based on an end-times theology not embraced by a majority of Christians." This is not a quote from the article, but appears rather as an editorial remark indicating the Standard's view of that series.

Evidently, writer Peter Chattaway, the author of the article was having his viewpoint supported by the weekly. Although the Editor of the paper, Marv Knox, replied to an email query that the publication of the article did not imply endorsement, he abstained from committing to a position *vis a vis* the direct question of his personal belief regarding the subject of the Lord's imminent trumpet cue. But, intriguingly, in a later *Down Home* [5] editorial reviewing the ongoing cultural battle in southern Baptist churches over wearing short pants to service, the editor did confess his fear of "flying off to heaven...in shorts and tennis shoes." At least his belief in the Rapture itself has, if inadvertently, been chronicled.

Letters to the editor 'for' and 'against' the Chattaway article did quickly follow in the ensuing issues of the weekly, many underlining the absurdity of believing these end-time prophecies. "Finally, we hear a clear response to Left Behind," cheered one reader from Fort Worth, TX, in favor of the critique.

"How long will it take for the evangelical world to wake up from the dreams of Hal Lindsey, John Walvoord, Dwight Pentecost and such 'luminaries'?" chimed in another commentator bolstering the article's observations. Another, from Commerce, TX, chided that as a teenager he had been scared stiff by books of this prophetical nature, though, "Now I am a little older and wiser."

In a reply, Dr. Thomas Ice, Pre-Trib Research Center, Arlington, TX, delved into the historical background apart from

Scripture per a biblical futurist viewpoint. "The novels teach items found in a significant number of the Anti-Nicene Fathers. We have found a pre-tribulation rapture statement dating back to the fourth century by one known as Pseudo-Ephraem. More significant for Texas Baptists is that a pre-tribulation rapture view was brought to the Colonies first by the father of American Baptist church history, Morgan Edwards, founder of Brown University. He taught a form of pre-tribulationism (sic) as early as 1744 and published his views in 1788. This is well before Darby." (Author: See Dr. Tim LaHaye's Harvest House publication, *The Rapture,* Chapter 12, for an introduction to 19th Century Bible teacher John Darby, who had such notable adherents as C.H. Spurgeon, D.L. Moody and C.I. Schofield.) Ice continues, "Dispensational beliefs have a better historical pedigree than is generally recognized by liberal scholarship."

Ice's article drew a response from one reader who had it on good authority that Mr. Ice held a collegiate stance that Jesus would return in 1988. Presumably error of that magnitude proves that the Lord's return is obviously far and away.

But even of those smaller percentages that accept the Rapture as doctrine, the largest number of these believes it is in the future. And of those that believe it will happen in the future, most of these seem to look for the Rapture to take place during or at the end of the tribulation. And within the smaller number that believe the Rapture will happen before the tribulation, the majority believes the tribulation or Apocalypse would then occur in some distant time, which makes the Rapture therefore still not in the immediate future. Ergo, the primary accepted position is that the Rapture is positively not imminent.

The inescapable conclusion: Few in the Body of Messiah expect the Rapture at any moment.

Scripture, nevertheless, teaches instead that the Rapture is not just near but is surely imminent. This is an event that shall take place at any moment. Before you have the opportunity to finish this sentence you are now reading, as an example. Actually, the speed of the event is even faster than that.

By what Godly authority shall we embark on this study? Ecclesiastes 1:13 [6] will do nicely to get us started. "And I set my heart to seek and search out by wisdom concerning all that is done under heaven, this burdensome task God has given to the sons of man, by which they must be exercised."

Eschatological statistics are available for all enamored of the particular, but the purpose of this study, again will be to focus on the overwhelming reality of how close is the Rapture. Somewhat like studying the coming birth of a child. There arrives a point when the attending nurses begin to stop watching the clock and start watching the mother to be.

One reason for writing this book is the realization that most Christians, and the world at large which is watching all those professing to be Christian, are becoming so caught up in the details of life that the Rapture has been relegated to the status of a future event. Not unlike planning for Christmas when Thanksgiving is at hand. Everyone basically knows when Thanksgiving is celebrated, and therefore it is a part of the schedule. Though none would suggest that the Rapture be fixed with a date, neither would many advise any kind of an actual watch for the Rapture be set in place. Why? The Rapture after all, is in the future. It's going to happen in God's time and therefore we need to get on with the business of life.

Yacov Rambsel, in his amazing study on the decoding of Scripture entitled, "The Genesis Factor,"[7] discerns a revealing juncture concerning the consideration of the Rapture. "Since the first century, God has given to every generation the same heavenly and holy calling on their lives. Be My Witnesses. But the statement, 'It is not for you to know the times or the seasons,' is being used today by some people who do not teach the Lord's imminent return to earth. They honestly believe it is not for us to know the times or the seasons for our day. However, I take exception to this thought, because the Bible plainly teaches us to be aware of the signs of the end of this age and to preach the Blessed Hope, the soon return of the Lord."

Parenthetically please note the phrasing of Pastor Rambsel's observation, which seemingly draws together the Rapture and the separately singular doctrine of the Return. These are distinctively individual occasions that shall be examined in the following chapter. Pastor Rambsel expertly defines important delineations between these two happenings in his fascinating documentation of the encoded affirmations of prophecy within prophecy. It is heartening to receive the enlightenment and consequent encouragement he bestows on the vital work of proclaiming the imminent aspect of the Rapture.

Notice Paul's admonition in I Thessalonians 4:17,[8] where the Apostle has been speaking of those who have died. He is striving to encourage believers who have loved ones who have fallen 'asleep' or as our finite minds behold, are dead.

In verse 17, Paul speaks to those believers who are still alive. "Then we who are alive and remain shall be caught up together with them in the clouds to meet the Lord in the air. And thus we shall always be with the Lord." Once again, parenthetically, note Paul is no longer alive. And though I do not have a death certificate for your perusal, I have been led to believe, by those who have studied these things in depth, that there are historical records describing Paul's death at a chopping block. No further sightings of import have been documented.

So did Paul miss a beat here? Was he suggesting that this Rapture would take place during his lifetime, and then miss the boat entirely and wind up dead before his prophecy could be fulfilled? This would align his prophecies on a par with the ilk of Jeanne Dixon, whose record was less than stellar.

A prophecy of the Lord's might clarify the intended meaning for us. Near the end of His final Passover celebration, Jesus, in prayer, remarks, "I do not pray for these alone. But for those who will believe in Me through their word: that they all may be one, as You, Father, are in Me, and I in You: that they also may be one in Us, that the world may believe that You sent Me." (John 17: 20-21) [9]

We shall observe but two points in this marvelous passage so enticingly deep. First, Jesus prays for all those that will believe in Him through the word of the disciples joined with Him at this Passover. As is well worth emphasizing, that would include all those who have followed Jesus by their act of acceptance of Him via the teachings of the apostles. That certainly would then include me, and

I prayerfully hope it also shall encompass each and every person that will read these words. And if you, personally, have not yet received the Lord, He will forgive your sins now, if you but ask. Believe on the Lord Jesus Christ and you too will be saved. (Romans 10:13) [10]

And may an interlinear note be observed. Do not overlook the brief yet glaring invitation just referenced. Two thoughts need expression here. One, the destiny of the Rapture, which this treatise is seeking to convey, is underscored, in comparison by the uniqueness of the plea given. In support, a second call includes within its' brevity the lateness of the hour. In Hebrews 3:7 [11] the reader finds, "Therefore, as the Holy Spirit says: Today, if you will hear his voice, do not harden your hearts as in the day of rebellion." Even the opportunity to eternal life here offered is impressively curt though still immediately and intentionally available.

Returning then to the primary discussion, a second point of focus is the fact that believers are one with Jesus and the Father. If you have just prayed this prayer, you also are now one with Jesus and the Father. That would make all of us one with the Apostle Paul. Being 'born again' causes us to begin to think in a new and supernatural way.

The promises and warnings of Scripture take on more glorious and ominous meanings as we shed the diminishing role of observer and suddenly are thrust into the arena as actor and participant.

Suddenly the very pages you hold are sensitized with a Holy power that is discernibly palpable. And with this perspective we return to Paul's pronouncement:

"Then we who are alive and remain shall be caught up..."

Yes, we are all running out of time. The time we have is merely what is remaining. Yes, we need the microseconds now. We must look into this moment, this startling, historical, prophetically power-charged 'Twinkling of an Eye,' which so soon shall come upon us. See there, I said, 'soon.'

Observe then how easy it is to fall into the future tense. To employ the word 'soon' in reference to the doctrine of the Rapture is a conflict of terminology. The word imminent means, 'impending, or any moment.' Catch your breath? It should. My desire is that by His grace, should He tarry, by the end of this study, these ponderings shall indeed give all readers of this viewpoint a cause to pause, and then look up!

CHAPTER II

Our Rapture, Then Messiah's Return

Tim LaHaye, pastor, teacher, writer and a visiting guest lecturer and commentator on Dr. David Breese's[12] TV Bible Prophecy study, 'The King Is Coming' telecast, just this afternoon spoke of looking forward to the Rapture. I was struck by the comment because I'd just finished sitting through a wonderful Gospel concert this morning in which many of the songs dealt with the Messiah's return. As Dr. LaHaye pointed out, there is a major difference between the Rapture and our Messiah's Return.

In the Rapture, Jesus will call out and meet believers in the air. On the other hand believers shall return to earth with Jesus at His Second Coming. In other words, the Rapture happens first and catches or snatches believers up into the sky to meet Jesus, who may or may not be seen by those that shall be left on earth due to their lack of acceptance of Jesus as Messiah.

The Return of Messiah then refers to Jesus' actually putting His foot on the Mount of Olives, who shall be a consummation of the prophecy, "…every eye shall see Him, even they who pierced Him.

And all the tribes of the earth shall mourn because of Him." (Revelation 1:7) [13]

What significance then is there in understanding the timing of the Rapture? Scripture informs us with several points of order that emerge in the Thessalonian passages we are considering that should be reckoned in this question.

First is the confrontation of death itself. The Thessalonian believers were beginning to be exposed to death firsthand, the first deaths experienced on a scale of appreciable measure since Jesus had ascended into heaven. This was not a part of the schedule, which they had understood would be included, in the teaching of His Return. But Paul attacked this disillusionment by commanding observance. "I do not want you to be ignorant brethren," he warned them, "concerning those who have fallen asleep, lest you sorrow as others who have no hope."[14]

Certainly Paul was not asking believers not to sorrow at the loss of those who experience death. In fact, the instruction goes, "Rejoice with those who rejoice, and weep with those who weep." (Romans 12:15) [15] The apostle's concern was for unseemly sorrow of the maudlin kind, that which gives over to despair. Jesus wept at Lazarus' death. The Jews even commented, "See how He loved him!" (John 11:36) [16]

Paul recognized that those who died without knowing the Lord, not having tasted of salvation, were truly those who have no hope. Do those people who have never heard truly need to worry about judgment? Paul is specific. Dying without Jesus as your Savior separates you from this life with no hope. There are no other options. No other possibilities. No other gods available. And there remains no oblivion or vast sea of nothingness upon which to sail away. "And as it is appointed for men to die once, but after this the judgment," is a statement which makes the reality of death and the ensuing obligations unavoidable. (Hebrews 9:27) [17]

But what of the sleep that is mentioned? This would be a description of passing beyond the veil. For Paul clearly teaches that absence from the body is presence with the Lord. And even in this portion we see that those who sleep in Jesus He will bring with Him at the Rapture. But there is no event from which to gage the closeness of the Rapture because this happening is 'imminent,' or any moment, whereas the Return prophesied in Matthew 24:29[18] is, '…immediately after the tribulation of those days…'

And it is because the Lord knows no event precedes the Rapture that He cautions vigilance to set a watch! "Watch therefore, and pray always that you may be counted worthy to escape all these things that will come to pass, and to stand before the Son of Man." (Luke 21:36) [19] This verse fits accordingly with Revelation 3:10,[20] "Because you have kept My command to persevere, I also will keep you from the hour of trial which shall come upon the whole world, to test those who dwell on the earth." And remember in I Thessalonians 5:8,[21] "For God did not appoint us to wrath, but to obtain salvation through our Lord Jesus Christ."

Observe that to be kept from the hour of trial that shall fall upon the whole world, one would need to have been *removed from the world entirely before hand*. Note the promise is to be kept 'from' not 'through' the hour.

"For if we believe that Jesus died and rose again, even so God will bring with Him those who sleep in Jesus."[22] Thus Paul returns to the central theme in which all scripture is anchored: The Gospel of Jesus Christ. And the Gospel is the death, burial and resurrection of *HaMashiach*, the Messiah. And if these things are believed, so should the other be known to be true. Conversely, should the Gospel be dispelled, what matter the rest of the tale.

And so then, knowing the Gospel is true, we understand the Rapture is as real as the nails that pierced His hands and feet. An impending prophecy shaped with the dimensions of eternal hope. The 'snatching away' is an event as unexpected and enigmatic as death. Yet, this 'Blessed Hope' remains as joyous in the hilarity of expectation as death is corrupting of the same. Two more perfect and larger opposites would be difficult to discern. One shall be as unending in its' beginning as the other is final in its' completion.

That an event so grand would be confined to so few lines in Scripture is worth note and further study. One can easily glean hidden jewels that abound throughout the pages of Holy Writ that continue to be slighted by ignorance while mankind strives to overcome his temporal and fleeting world.

A reality is impending upon us of which even death has no order for those who believe. It is known as the Rapture and will precede Christ's return to the earth. How soon will the event transpire? It is not in the future. It is imminent. Any moment. And it shall be 'in the twinkling of an eye.' (I Corinthians 15:52) [23]

Jesus said His yoke would be easy. So a gentle reminder for this aspect of the doctrine of The Lord's Return might be suggested as –Our Rapture, Then Messiah's Return.

CHAPTER III

Abide In Jesus

The company founded by Thomas Alva Edison developed an experiment to time the twinkling of an eye. It would be interesting to discover what prompted the engineers at General Electric to promote such a test. Dr. Jack Van Impe[24] has often quoted the results of this test as being 11/100's of a second. That is evidently how quickly a light beam moves through the eye in what is identified as a 'twinkle.'

Lest anyone conclude these considerations as toying with the trivial, the interjection of a few major points from an article that appeared online at abcnews.go.com may here be inveighed. Beneath the headline, "Measuring Time With Light,"[25] July 12, 2001, reporter Amanda Onion chronicles the unveiling of the latest, most accurate timepiece extant.

"A New Clock Records Time a Million Billion Times a Second," the subheading informs the reader. Ms. Onion continues, "The most accurate clocks today slip by only one second every 30 million years. For scientists at the National Institute of Standards and Technology in Boulder, Colo., that's just not accurate enough.

"Instead, they've built a clock designed to only slip by a second once every 30 billion years. This clock (which would never fit on the wrist, since it takes up the size of a large lab room) records time by counting the rapid-fire oscillations in a laser. The oscillations, in turn, are kept in pace by a single mercury atom that vibrates at a constant cadence. The result is a clock that counts time by the femtosecond –a million-billionth's of a second."

Ms. Onion goes on to detail the marvelous workings of this new fangled timepiece and strides leading to its' development. But suffice it to note that with that kind of accuracy being engineered, surely we can entertain the modest study of the twinkling of an eye, which postulates into a relatively lazy 11/100's of a second!

And for those that might judge such scientific calculations as infantile in perspective and void of value, a couple thoughts are worth entering here.

Recent studies are suggesting that there are in fact speeds superior to that which is traveled by light. Without entering the controversy, it does Christians well to remember that Jesus described Himself as '...the light...' (John 8:12) [26] A statement in itself that reveals, *if speeds exist faster than light*, one might easily go so fast that the substance is missed while striving to attain the vain.

The more sobering and profitable consideration is that offered in I Corinthians 15:51-52,[27] "Behold, I tell you a mystery: We shall not all sleep, but we shall all be changed –in a moment, in the twinkling of an eye, at the last trumpet. For the trumpet will sound, and the dead will be raised incorruptible, and we shall be changed." There it is again. This time we have the Rapture in a nutshell.

First we note that we shall not all sleep. Remember the exhortation in the Thessalonian passage that informs us that when Jesus calls us out the dead in Christ shall rise first? They are the ones referred to as those who are asleep.

So here we are bedazzled by the prophecy that not all believers are going to die! Although, "...it is appointed for men to die once, but after this the judgment," Hebrews 9:27 [28] God's power is displayed in the realization that He, being the Divine Appointment Maker, is quite capable of being also the Divine Appointment Breaker. It might even be more proper to recognize that in God's daily planner there are appointments and then there are *appointments*!

And one of the most fundamental of expectancies on any actuarial chart worth its' salt is being adjusted before our very eyes as we behold the eternal realities of God. Not everyone's chart is going to have the death block checked. The place is there, the appointment is set, but the ink will never touch the spot. That space will be left blank for some who will be Raptured, or caught away. A concept referenced even from the Latin of Jerome's Vulgate,[29] *'rapio'* translated 'snatch away.'

"Oh death where is thy sting, O Hades thy victory?" (I Cor. 15:55 [30] –Hosea 13:14[31])

And then we read not only are believers not going to die but these same believers, caught up to be with the Lord, are going to be changed. "And as we have borne the image of the man of dust, we shall bear the image of the heavenly Man." (I Cor. 15:49) [32] This last reference obviously to that tantalizing encouragement from the Apostle John in I John 3:2 [33] "Beloved, now we are children of God, and it has not yet been revealed what we shall be, but we know that when He is revealed, we shall be like Him, for we shall see Him as He is." And this is the image, His image, into which we are going to be changed for eternity.

This change will take place at the last trump. Not to be confused with the last trump of Revelation that deals with judgments all of which are preceded by signs and wonders that are delineated and therefore definable as they take place. This trump which Paul calls to our attention is the certain and final sound of the gathering of all believers back to the Lord. An example as given by the Roman army on the order for the military units to 'move out.' The last trumpet, of a series, that is given to put a stationary force on the move. Trumpet one: Break Camp. Trumpet Two: Assemble to March. Trumpet Three: (The Last Trump) Move Out!

And perhaps a more intriguing hint was given the Children of Israel when God commanded Moses, saying, "Make two silver trumpets for yourself; you shall make them of hammered work; you shall use them for calling the congregation and for directing the movement of the camps. (Numbers 10:2) [34]

You've heard of the noise that wakes the dead? Well, that is exactly what this final trumpet blast shall do. Or will the sound emanate from a *shofar*? Whichever instrument, the dead in Christ shall be raised first. And they shall be instantaneously converted into their incorruptible, eternal bodies! And then we who remain shall also be changed instantaneously as we are caught up to be with the Lord! And ever shall we be with the Lord!

And in striving to save the best for last, as Jesus so often did, we focus once again on the most spectacular element of this prophecy, the condensing of time to the nearly infinitesimal twinkling of an eye.

Behold the elapsed space of time: 11/100's of a second. That encompasses the inauguration of this momentous occasion. A moment recognized to be so microscopic that a test under laboratory conditions had to be applied to help define the parametric blueprint of the event's borders.

Should we describe a change of equal proportions from the natural to the supernatural, from the finite to the infinite, from the temporal to the eternal, a span of several million years would go unchallenged as logical to the proportion of change described. The Darwinian perspective for one comes to mind.

And as to this revolutionary understanding of instantaneous change, even God, throughout the *Tanakh*, the Old Testament of Christianity, continually encouraged those who followed Him, to wait upon Him.

Yet, there is a moment coming dear reader, flashing down upon us with the speed unimaginable to our finite minds, in which the most monumental progression in the history of mankind is going to be manifested. In a moment, in the twinkling of an eye, it shall occur and be finished. Faster than you can catch your breath this shall be. And it will take place instantaneously following the shout of the Lord and a trumpet blast.

So we can see that this teaching of imminence does not cause us to become less responsive to God's earthly ministry but more. It is more necessary to abide in Him as we strive to be obedient to His command to watch than ever before. "Thou wilt keep him in perfect peace, whose mind is stayed on Thee: because he trusteth in Thee." (Is. 26:3) [35]

CHAPTER IV

History Is His Story

In speaking with a Christian leader, a pastor and teacher, I was amazed to discover that he was reluctant to offer a position on the Rapture. Hebrews 9:28 [36] makes plain God's desired attitude and order for those considering this momentous occasion. "...To those who eagerly wait for Him He will appear a second time, apart from sin, for salvation." Of course, then, we must weigh with emphasis the New King James offering, '...to those who *eagerly* wait for Him He will appear..."

Mark your most recent experience that enthused eagerness. It may have been a new car. Perhaps it was the anticipation of a wedding? Whatever the event, you can recall it with ease. You were 'eager' for the consideration to become a reality. Eager, no confusion in that description is there? Yet the instruction to eagerness in expecting this event has throughout the Body of Messiah over the centuries been dulled down in the least and completely eradicated in the main.

Seeing my amazement that he was not actually forthcoming in this particular area of consideration, the elderly 'Statesman' of the Body offered by way of explanation that his lifelong focus had been on history. Echoing in my mind was the remark of my first pastor, a man without formal seminary training, who observed, "Education is life." It was from this pastor also that I first heard that 'History is His Story.' Jesus said, "I am the way, the truth and the life. No one comes to the Father except through Me." (John 14:6) [37] And His story is only just begun. So it may be propitious here to recall that though those who refuse to study history may be relegated to repeat it, the other side of that coin may then well be that whosoever becomes engulfed in history endangers their ability to respond to the imminent.

Thus this study focuses on only one solitary moment in His story that shall once again shatter the understanding of mankind. So eternally vast is truth and so fragile is man's comprehension.

And the return of the Bridegroom to whisk away His Bride portends to be a significant part of His story. Jesus even told a parable which dealt with 10 virgins waiting for their bridegroom. Five were wise and five were foolish. Five were prepared and went into the wedding supper. Five were not ready and found the door closed to their entrance. "Watch therefore," Jesus warned, "for you know neither the day nor the hour in which the Son of Man is coming." (Matthew 25:13) [38] If Jesus here was speaking of His stepping onto the Mount of Olives at the end of the seven-year tribulation as many Bible scholars believe, then how much more prepared should the Christian be to hear the shout of the Lord?

These observations certainly agree with Scripture's descriptions of Jesus. In fact not only did Jesus call Himself 'the life,' but Revelation 19:10 [39] delves even more deeply into His Person by fashioning the statement, "For the testimony of Jesus is the spirit of prophecy." This last borne out by recognizing that all Scripture is directly connected to the Messiah and His work and subordinated to it.

And of His work there are few prophecies that so completely encompass the entire body of believers' involvement as the Rapture. And as we have seen in the last chapter, Jesus Himself ordered a watch set so that we would be prepared for the events of the last days. No wonder the Apostle Paul would utter a similar command in I Thessalonians 5:6,[40] "Therefore let us not sleep, as others do, but let us watch and be sober." Then in verse 9 of that chapter, the Apostle assures us, "For God did not appoint us to wrath, but to obtain salvation through our Lord Jesus Christ."

Lastly, in verse 11 Paul reiterates his reasoning from verse 18 of the preceding chapter in dealing with the topic of the Rapture and the events of the end times, "Therefore comfort one another with these words."[41]

So we of this present age can understand as we look back over the past two millenniums that a doctrine was established to keep us aware of approach of the events of the end. That we should be able to define our position to at least some degree, heeding the warning not to be ignorant concerning eschatology or the doctrine of the study of last things.

And retrospectively, we can also easily observe that as the apostles looked forward all prophecies intertwined to be connected on the string of lights which when empowered by the Holy Spirit spell out first and foremost: Jesus The Messiah *shall return.*

As far away into the past as the times of Isaiah, God was pointing to the end of the ages. Reiterations Paul and other Apostles would echo in the New Testament teachings, we read, "Wail, for the Day of the Lord is at hand! It will come as destruction from the Almighty. Therefore all hands will be limp, every man's heart will melt, And they will be afraid. Pangs and sorrows will take hold of them; they will be in pain as a woman in childbirth; they will be amazed at one another; their faces will be like flames. Behold the Day of the Lord comes, cruel, with both wrath and fierce anger, to lay the land desolate, and He will destroy its sinners from it. For the stars of heaven and their constellations will not give their light; the sun will be darkened in its light to shine." (Isaiah 13:6-10) [42]

Immediately the prophecy we had been considering that teaches believers are not appointed unto wrath becomes soothing. Comfort begins to ooze from that promise in these lightning flashes of Isaiah's warnings we have just struggled through.

Should we dig deeper into these types of end time prophecies, and all those who may should do so toward their own sobering, we'd surely discover the predictions becoming more dire and bleak, not less.

Watch care for impending historical events is suddenly not such a foolish idea. Did we miss our turn, or is anyone watching the road?

Rapture departure time takes on its' own significance in light of these forewarnings. Recognition of the reality of the truth of the event is momentarily warmed to mild interest in the very least. A position paper on the placement in the schedule of impending prophecies appears as not unperceptive preparation.

Even casual stoical observation becomes encouraged. Crowds, instead of dissipating at the mention of the last day conversations, actually begin to solidify and, dare it be suggested, grow?

In his following Chapter Five, Paul deals with the day of the Lord. The apostle has just finished Chapter Four with the admonition to, "…comfort one another with these words." [43] He then opens by separating the two prophetical happenings with a marked sea change in verse 1,[44] "But, concerning the times and the seasons, brethren, you have no need that I should write to you." Ah, course change. Here the reader discovers the Thessalonians are not in complete ignorance. They know some things. Paul turns to a new subject and new contemplations.

In verse two, he identifies, "For you yourselves know perfectly that the day of the Lord so comes as a thief in the night." He addresses not the same subject he has been writing about in the previous passage. No, he is not continuing the same course of discussion. The Rapture, again, has no prophetical parameters. There are no issues or distinctions for which we should be watching. We must then be alert for the event itself.

The Day of the Lord, however, has events before, during and even after which parenthetically set it apart as so many earlier prophecies did, i.e., the birth of Jesus, etc. And the most prominent prophecy to begin that day appears to be the Rapture.

Verse three, "For when they say, "Peace and safety!' then sudden destruction comes upon them, as labor pains upon a pregnant woman. And they shall not escape." This prophesied false peace and safety falls upon the earth following the Rapture, not before the Blessed Hope occurs. A certain obvious havoc shall descend upon society immediately following the moment of

Rapture. Adding to a plate overflowing, the ensuing chaos will increase the demand for a leader to be brought forth. One European has already been quoted that such a man shall be followed, "...whether he be devil or angel."[45] He shall make war like no other. Victorious, his efforts shall in reality muster but a brittle order and peace, weak imitation only. And then...

At the risk of seeming heavy-handed, might we mark that first of all the deceived shall be yearning for 'peace and safety' from any quarter. Bedlam resulting in the instantaneous disappearance of even possibly millions upon millions of humans coupled with whatever other consequent disasters may trouble the day will undoubtedly cause a corporate desire for peace with safety as good measure. (Blessed are the peacemakers, right?) And they shall not be disappointed, at least initially. The announcement of victory shall come! And then the ball of twine shall begin to unravel in terrifying jolts. Observing the comparison to the woman and the allegorical course of birth pangs, we are once again reminded of frail efforts to blunt our conceit at time keeping.

And then finally, with the prophesy that will end all prophecy concerning judgment, we are informed that, '...and they shall not escape."[46]

How is that last statement for finality? No escape. That'll preach. No Rapture to follow. "Watch therefore, and pray always that you may be counted worthy to escape all these things that shall come to pass, and to stand before the Son of Man." Jesus said in Luke 21:36.[47]

It should be noted parenthetically that in Walvoord's labyrinthine work, "Every Prophecy of the Bible," this last verse somehow escaped that author's consideration. In fact, the whole of Luke 21:34-38 is absent.[48]

"And there will be signs in the sun, in the moon, and in the stars, and on the earth distress of nations, with perplexity, the sea and the waves roaring; men's hearts failing them from fear and the expectation of those things which are coming on the earth, for the powers of the heavens will be shaken. Then they will see the Son of Man coming in a cloud with power and great glory. Now when these things begin to happen, look up and lift up your heads, because your redemption draws near." (Luke 21:25-28) [49]

So there is escape? We can watch for the signs? No. These things shall happen after the Rapture takes place. In fact, these are the closing moments of this world's age. Jesus' Return is what is being revealed. A specific encouragement to endure to the end is being made. Those looking up have survived the last half of the seven-year tribulation. Remember, the signs and wonders. But no sign is offered in Paul's description of the Rapture.

These signs are during the tribulation. Afterwards, the Son of Man shall be seen, coming to the earth. Before the tribulation ensues, those may only see Jesus who shall be snatched out of the world, when He comes to the sky and the trumpet is sounded. And there are no signs for this. Only sounds are given. A shout followed by a trumpet blast is the only prompt of this historic occasion. The 'head's up' (literally, ha-ha!) shall be only for those in Christ. 'Come up hither,' per Revelation 4:1,[50] shall be the only command. The call shall be given, as in Numbers 10,[51] and the sound of a voice like a trumpet for the 'assembly' (the word used in Acts 4:38,[52] also translated as 'congregation' in some versions and 'church' in others) to be gathered together.

Ready? Remember, the 'any moment' is the span of time recorded as 11/100's of a second. Imminent. Watching? And are we listening for the shout, also? That precedes the trumpet, which may combine with the shout to gain our attention to look up and see Him!

CHAPTER V

Information Overload

We have now entered the generation of 'Information Overload.' Cell phone wrong numbers in rush hour traffic. Business lunches gobbled up behind the wheel from fast food pit stops. Heartburn begins just thinking. We have stopped running out of time. Now we're re-inventing it. Multi-tasking and overlays of responsibility are now the rule for jobs with expandable and retractable job descriptions.

Now we have employment agencies for long-term temp to perm career building. You're hired by a temp agency to work as outsource labor for an international conglomerate that, if you pass muster and qualify by staying the allotted course prescribed, has allowed that they 'may' hire you, perhaps, maybe.

Meanwhile, the international conglomerate conferences with the national government agencies to support outsource needs by offering a permanently temporary labor supply. This cost effective labor initiative enhances margins and defrays costs while avoiding expenditures. International borders melt as companies across the earth vie for technical staff in a mad scramble to stay ahead of the curve that is as indiscernible behind as it is ahead.

It's as if we were studying pages of statistics on a wall only to find we have suddenly become enveloped in those stats and now are lost inside of them. I find my mechanic watching the news from Wall Street while talking on his cell phone when I enter his shop to get my car's scheduled oil change. As he changes the oil we discuss the spread of hundreds of dollars in difference between the various shops I've requested estimates from for work on a special problem with the car. I finally settled on the lowest bid, $76 versus the highest bid of $753 plus change.

My mechanic gets into an argument over the disposal of the used oil with one of his helpers. I don't get the resolve because the argument is in an Indian dialect. As I stand by the auto waiting for the mechanic to open the garage door before I climb in to back the vehicle out, he motions for me to begin moving the car. I point out that the door is yet unopened. Embarrassed, he reminds me that he's waiting because it is cold outside. He wants me to back up as close to the door as possible because then he will only have to open the door for a shorter period of time. Now I'm embarrassed at my lack of sensitivity. I jump in and back up to the door. He pulls the door open. There's a truck parked right in front of the door. A flurry of Indian dialects erupts in challenges and recriminations. Finally someone goes out and moves the truck. A small battle lost early in the day, the mechanic watches me back out and then turns dejectedly back into the garage. It's the small things that are causing the defeats in this day and age.

The great battles, the important ones, go largely ignored, unnoticed or stagnant. Close to 45 million babies have been butchered in unthinkable procedures in America, so ghastly in their aspect that describing the acts makes the reporter feel a breach of etiquette has been committed. A more comprehensible grasp of this horrific slaughter comes to mind from the roadside memorial billboard entering Corpus Christi, Texas, which bears the statistic, "150 babies die through abortion every hour in America." Anyone who would advertise these details of such atrocities is publicized to be a wretch of the most sordid kind. Otherwise, how could they dwell on these evil and morbid views that insult one by the very reading. And thus pro-life advocates with pictures that evidence the thousands of atrocities being performed every day across America become the perpetrators of abomination. Conversely, all who believe each person has the right to choose to kill his or her own child, as long as that person does not reveal pictures resulting from their choice then become our champions and our new heroes to fete.

And heroes are desperately needed here. In his monthly letter of June 11, 2001, Coral Ridge Pastor Dr. D. James Kennedy[53] published new reports of the escalation in murdering children. Babies considered unworthy of life are left to die after birth. He includes the testimony of a Chicago area nurse who held an abandoned down syndrome boy, shunted off to the Soiled Laundry Utility Room because his parents did not want to hold him and because no one else had time to care for him either. The nurse held the boy for 45 minutes until he finally succumbed. Dr. Kennedy[54] confesses becoming "aghast to learn a prominent bio-ethicist at Princeton University, another of the Ivy League schools such as Harvard founded to train preachers of the Gospel, is now going so far as to argue that doctors should be free to exterminate children up to 28 days of age if they are deemed expendable because of medical problems." Exterminate? Adolph Hitler would have loved this man.

A report surfaced recently of a group of activists on both sides of the abortion issue being brought together to defuse the tensions after a doctor of abortion was himself murdered. Led by a Roman Catholic archbishop, the group agreed to use terms that would not incite hostility. Words like 'abortion' were nixed, and others changed, such as 'unborn baby' to fetus, Latin for 'unborn child.' Obviously, anyone with the pictures of actual abortions would not make the cut for this group. Evidently, one must draw the line somewhere.

The figure for total abortions in the past several decades across the earth is unavailable. China and Russia separately would dwarf the numbers of America's approximate 45 million dead. Actually the figures must be continually revised upward by roughly 1.5 million per annum just in America. At the beginning of 2001 the figure was roughly 39 million plus. That would mean as of this update, August of 2004, the total would be around 45 million give or take a baby. For more exact figures contact D. James Kennedy's Coral Ridge Ministries in Florida or Operation Save America's Flip Benham.[55] An example of the acuteness of the problem was the necessity for a ruling at the Nice, France 2001 EU conference of the same name in which it was determined to affirm that unborn children have no right to life. Protests were few and mild in rendition. For historians the first official legal position in America was the famed 'Dred Scott' decision made by the 1857–8 U.S. Supreme Court in which Blacks were characterized as non-persons. The Jews suffered the same legal status under Hitler. Of course, Jews are still characterized thusly in the Moslem culture, but then Islam relegates all unbelievers to the position of infidel anyway. On the other hand, Jesus said in Mark 16, "...he that believeth not (the Gospel) shall be damned."[56] So the conclusion and Good News is that there shall be a reckoning. In the mean time as they used to say in Viet Nam, a body count is once again in order. The 10-year Viet Nam war cost over 58,000 lives. Doing the math then, there have been roughly 775 Nam's for the unborn babies of America. Who in America would stand for 775 Viet Nam's? Answer: The Majority Rules.

Of course it only becomes murkier when one realizes that the aborted babies are sold, often before they are ripped or burned from their mothers' wombs'. And should they be brought out whole and intact, their sellers win top dollar. Six hundred per corpse was the going price in recent years on a published sheet of baby body parts price lists.[57] And that was in Irving, TX. What might the babes bring on the hoof in the larger metropolitan areas of the world? These sale prices are of course also outdated. Ah, the world of commerce!

One nurse in the Irving, TX, area reported her horror at watching twins drowned in a bucket to keep their bodies unharmed. At least they died together one might eulogize.

And the UN is working on legislation to ensure that anti-abortion positions shall become outside the law. (See Concerned Women for America, www.cwfa.org.)[58] It puts a whole new spin on UNESCO's chartered motto which proclaims, 'the children are ours.' It must be concluded by the legislation that the motto's intent is obvious.

One barely remembers the anti-abortion movie, "Silent Scream." So surprisingly unaccepted, so quickly forgotten. But then, people are supposed to want real movies. Snuff movies they are called. Shudders begin in the depths of the mind at what will ensue from this point should our Lord tarry.

Returning to the forefront of science, speaking in an embryonic fashion, the new controversy is cloning. Selective breeding. Does that practice ring any bells for history buffs?

And here we are again. How quickly we forget. And there we see it above us, the doctrine of the imminent, looming out of the mists of higher ground. Oh, how refreshing a breeze! Is it any wonder the Rapture is designated Our Blessed Hope? Elevation out of the morass brings tears of relief and joyous Hallelujahs!

Though admittedly the Rapture will bring its' own momentary havoc, militarily described as collateral damage. Planes will drop from the sky. Cars, trucks, tractors and motorcycles will be just a sampling of the traffic vehicles wrecking. Anyone in the tow business will make a killing. Resulting gridlock will go beyond comprehension. Those at sea shall not escape. Importantly, some captains and members of their crews will also vanish upward. Passengers, more or less, shall not be as problematic in their disappearances. And the train wrecks, of course, will be as inevitable as the last chorus in the proverbial country song. And these calamities shall be showered across the world. Though there shall be Rapture induced problems few and far between in Islamic countries. Their problems will arise later with the coming of the Antichrist and his demand they worship him as God. That also will not be a happy story. Where Christian leaders reign societies shall suffer greater initial impact and confusion at the evacuation of the Bride. Words are accountably inadequate.

Lives of most left behind will be devastated by the Rapture. Presumably there will be many, such as those in the New Age movement, which will rejoice at the erasure of the narrow minded, ill educated Christians that God, in His and Her Mercy, has finally dispensed with.

Some, including a majority of Christians, believe the Rapture as taught by futurists includes a mysterious aspect. This is described as the 'secret' Rapture. An invisible spontaneously instantaneous vanishing of millions of humans is a hard idea to get the mind around when so much publicity on this prophecy has already gone forth, even in these last few decades. The confusion seems to be connected with the continuing refusal of the majority of professing Christians to accept the pre-millennial interpretation of eschatology. Evidently, being able to push all prophecy into the future eases the burden of having to deal with God's warning of 'while it is still called today.'

Hindsight is invariably more accurate than foresight. Untold billions of citizens of planet earth shall experience the Rapture as witnesses. Here's an encouragement of sorts. Even if you are not saved, you at least are going to be in attendance for one of the all-time Great Happenings of History! Yes, that the event would happen unobserved on such a massive scale across the earth is tough to conceptualize.

Speaking of which, what will cameras film at the Fast Take? With all the security cams around the world, surely there will be footage worth viewing. Will the tapes leave a trace of the Big Twinkle? Will all the governments of the world quickly scramble to destroy any evidence of the Rapture? What will the film capture at a speed of 11/100's of a second? There's another intriguing problem to mull over, what to do with all the film that captures any evidence of our Home Going? One is reminded of the TV world news report back in the early 90's. Viewers glimpsed an earthquake bouncing a man out of bed in a newsroom in Japan. And the room dissembling around him in chaos was a prophetic preview similar to scenes out of the later released 'Twister.'[59] Will there be a time of transition over several days? Logically and more probable the transition period will last more like weeks or months. Even if you don't believe this, how long is it going to take for you to forget the reality of the Rapture once it has taken the Bride out of the world?

Will the world watch reruns of millions upon millions of people jetting into the sky in glorified bodies, in the same way TV viewers sat transfixed for days watching the World Trade Towers collapse over and over again on channel after channel day after day?

Did you see the news item about the doctor that was operating on a mother who was two to three months from delivering her baby? A cameraman was present filming the doctor at work. The doctor had made an incision in the mother's womb. Just before the doctor began to close the womb, a tiny hand reached out and began to feel around in the air, fingers wiggling. The cameraman would later say the experience convinced him that babies are alive in the womb. Evidently, he had not been of that persuasion before the filming took place. A tiny hand waving from inside its' mother's womb bespeaks so much life as to be indescribable in a single phrase.

The wave lasted several seconds before the doctor gently guided the hand back inside the mother, in order to sew up the incision. A filmed shot of only a few seconds was recorded. And that baby's wave was seconds longer than the twinkling of an eye that clocks in at a fraction of the speed, to be sure. That God-breathed moment won't even take a second, or a quarter, or an eighth, or a sixteenth. Do you see the micro distance that must be traversed to arrive at the miniscule? It's over before we get there. Are you ready?

Do you know Jesus? "For 'whoever calls on the name of the Lord shall be saved.'" (Romans 10:13) [60] You should have time right now to call upon the Lord. Notice that I wrote 'should'? Maybe I'm finally gaining the right perspective. Won't you make certain?

One man prayed in the temple. He couldn't even lift his eyes to God he felt so condemned. All he could pray was, "Lord have mercy on me, a sinner." (Luke18: 13) [61]

You too may be justified in the eyes of God. It takes just over two seconds to utter that prayer, though it may include a lifetime to reach its' pronouncement. Two seconds is about the length of time that baby used to wave to the world. Just over two seconds is not a long time, is it? In fact it seems absurdly short to represent a door to eternity, wouldn't you agree? Still, as brief a moment as it is, it's not so brief as 11/100's of a second.

Now that's a small door. Or should it be described rather as 'narrow'?

CHAPTER VI

Rapture Fast

Telling time has been a challenge for man since the Garden of Eden. Not having enough time is often not the real problem. But, as in the Garden, the true problem more often is having too much time. And then suddenly you're in a place where you have time on your hands and temptation in your way. You have all the answers but you don't like any of them and you're not really sure they are the right answers anyway. Who knows? Quien Sabe?

Saving time is often equated with gaining speed, which offers the illusion of controlling time. Like so much in life, the rate of movement is relational.

On a mission trip to Alaska this writer had the opportunity to take the twelve-hour ride by train from Anchorage to Fairbanks. After the train pulled out of the station, the conductor came down the aisle punching tickets. He was asked when the train would pick up speed. Furrowing his brow the conductor noted that the train was at top speed. The enquirer pressed on to say that this scheduled trip was billed as the 'express.' You're in Alaska," the conductor began closing the conversation, "Where did you want to go?"

Wealth is equally deceptive. A young pastor, and his wife were invited to dine with a wealthy oilman at his lakeside home. During the meal the pastor's wife shared her day's activities that included paying bills of 10, 20 and various dollar increments. She then wondered what her host's day had been like. He agreed his time had been spent in much the same way, seeking to pay bills, 10 million here, twenty million there.

Knowledge gains no additional perspective. In fact Paul warns that knowledge 'will vanish away.' (I Corinthians 13:8) [62]

Time itself continues 'swifter than a weaver's shuttle' we read in Job, and then suddenly life is over, past, someone has 'gone on.' (Job 7:6) [63]

Amazingly, we have reached a level of sophistication in society that we are often no longer surprised by death. In fact, fans of Woody Allen movies, as an example, accept that death can and often is an inevitable theme in his films. But art can blueprint more of life, even before the fact of dying, a la 'China Syndrome' *vis a vis* Three Mile Island. But we'll take a closer look at that later, if we have time.

Alicia

She was intelligent and friendly, a quick wit with a ready smile, and always willing to lend an ear.

We met in training class, in a group of a couple dozen people accepted to receive an eight-week course to qualify for entrance into an international company. She had just recently been married.

We got through the course with most of those we started with and began employment. Within a year she had become with child and lost it. Then within another year she and her husband were blessed with child, and a little girl was born, her husband was promoted and they moved to another city. Life was good. They were following a real estate agent to look at a new house when they came to a notoriously dangerous intersection of that city. Citizens had long been lobbying for traffic lights at this spot. Accidents here were well known by locals for being frequent and bad. Besides, it was a government town and fast lane living was the rule rather than the exception, so the light could wait. The real estate agent made his turn and the husband followed suit keeping up. A motorist in a hurry sped through the adjacent stop sign while the couple's vehicle was crossing the T. She and the baby girl were in the back seat. The husband was alone in the front. Fastened securely into her infant car seat, the little girl was not anchored to the auto's seatbelt. Mom was not wearing a seat belt either. Life was good. They were on their way to see the new house.

When the oncoming vehicle slammed into the couple's car broadside Alicia and the baby were blasted out the rear window onto the pavement and both killed instantly. The husband awoke in the hospital two days later, unaware of what had happened and his tragic loss, suffering only minor injuries.

It's not the way things are supposed to work. But often it is exactly the way life happens. We have our ducks all lined up. They're all quacking in unison, in step and headed in a line in the desired direction. We are in the perfect picture. Or we're on the way to the perfect picture. What could happen?

(Must include this parenthetical report. Am now working on the second draft of this study. Things have been going well. Celebrated Resurrection Sunday this morning and since the church is in holiday gear, we will be home this evening. Feeling refreshed, I began working on the manuscript. The family was in the living room watching a documentary on the new facts developing in the case of the 'Shroud of Turin.' Got caught returning to the family room after getting a glass of water and began watching the documentary because it relates to a book I've been reading by Dr. Grant R. Jeffrey, one of the leading prophecy scholars on the planet extant, in which he devotes one chapter to the 'Shroud' studies. Couldn't resist comparing the documentary findings with Dr. Grant's work in *Jesus, the Great Debate*.[64] Heard noise in the family room and discovered Samuel, our youngest, just a few months away from his fourth birthday, hard at work on the computer. It took my wife Karen several agonizing minutes to restore the manuscript, minus the seven or so pages of work from this afternoon. We were grateful not more was lost. I took a nap and they all went for a walk. After returning, Samuel came and put his arms around my neck and whispered in my ear, "Dad, I'm sorry I messed with the computer." It almost made it worth it. Picking back up with 'Alicia' completed the sense of the thing. Why? Began again with the paragraph that ends with, "What could happen?")

Saw the movie "Left Behind," based on the Rapture, just the other night. One film character is well-known TV actor Clarence Gilyard. He is a Christian in real life. Anyway, the movie is out on video and is scheduled for release in a few months on the silver screen. In a shrewd step to heighten public interest while financing the film's theatrical debut the producers, Peter and Paul La Londe, seeded the video field first. (Those months have since flown by, the movie premiered and went into distribution and the pan has flashed. Little ado was even made within the Christian community, much less in the world at large. But in fairness, in the high-speed world of today any effort must make gargantuan impact to garner even the briefest of attentions.)

Today Mr. Gilyard was a co-host on a nationally televised Thanksgiving Day Parade show. He was playing himself. There were several parades across the country. The quick witted among you have already guessed what day this is that is taking place.

My oldest son, Daniel, is nine now and in the living room watching the first airing of "It's A Wonderful Life" of the season. He's really enjoying it. It's still new to him, since he's only seen it once or twice before.

As George Bailey's breakdown scene at home, "Will you stop playing that stupid piano?" materializes I can sense a new quietness envelope the living room. Danny and I had just finished a confrontation before the movie began which sounds eerily reminiscent of the frantic tones Jimmy Stewart is empowering his character with. The frustration, panic and overwhelming desperation were all three in our scene but ours' was not a movie. Art imitating life, or once again, how real can things become? And how fast can things get?

I'm not sure when this book is going to be finished and when it will be out. If it follows the film version of "Left Behind" it may be touted as an also ran. There certainly could be a spate of books on the Rapture.

(Again, the film has since premiered. No excitement or reaction was noticed outside the Christian community, and comparatively little within it. To be fair, it was a good movie, and makes an even better sermon. The acting was excellent. The courage to embark on this subject is admirable in the very least. The directing was invisible. And seeing preachers that have proclaimed the truth of the Rapture for decades such as Jack Van Impe and his wife and John Hagee and his spouse play in the very moment of the Rapture scene was absolutely delightful to all who hold the Blessed Hope! But the shallowness of response merely supports the line of this book that the Rapture is a doctrine not seriously entertained by those professing to believe in the Lord. I suppose I should be flattered if not happy. Also, it is the firm belief of this writer, by way of observation, that each of these repetitions in life enforces the human understanding that basically all things often appear to remain the same.)

The ease with which most of us can be lulled into complacency argues effectively against any perceived pattern in life that would seem to bear significance. Sameness also dampens the argument for absolutism, which conveniently makes way for encouragement to acknowledge other beliefs, and perhaps a little exploration or drifting away...or is that rather falling away?

By the time the movie hits the theatres we should have a new President. Certainly that should give you a clue as to the year this is being written. (The winner by a TKO.) Read an editorial on the net today about the origin of Thanksgiving. Many versions are claiming that the Indians saved the pilgrims and the pilgrims threw a party to thank the Indians. So much for history as fact...

Historical questions now have to do with TV schedules, sports records and favorite songs. Not much wonder that the country is in such confusion.

There's a Special coming up on one of the public stations of a religious celebration at the UN. All the religions of the world shall be worshiping together. Except of course Christianity. Oh, the World Council of Churches is represented. But there are not any groups that are exclusivist. You know, the ones that believe you must know Jesus to go to heaven. Only the Christians that know that their religion is not any better than everyone else's are invited. These are not the Christians guest speaker for this holy soiree, Ted

Turner, remembers from his childhood. We all know how important it is to exclude exclusivists in the spirit of inclusiveness.

Remember the game of tag you used to play when you were a child. There was always a home base. You could touch it and be safe from being tagged. Some believe our lives are like that. You can go anywhere you like. And you may believe what you want. Do or say as you please. As long as you can get back to home base before you're tagged you're safe. Trouble is, home base has been eliminated. There are no absolutes, or so children are being taught. But tag is not nearly as much fun without a home base. And you're never free.

As God has said, "...Come out from among them and be separate, says the Lord, do not touch what is unclean, and I will receive you." (II Corinthians 6:16-17) [65]

How fast are you? Can you really change directions in 11/100's of a second? Have you ever thought you could be that fast? Paul instructs that we who believe in Jesus the Messiah shall imminently be moved that quickly. The idea has been offered in description as the Church being 'snatched away.' Through His Grace and Power, the Rapture is prophesied to be that fast. Notice I didn't say 'this fast.' However, when 'that' becomes 'this' then of course, 'this' shall become 'that.' Ready?

CHAPTER VII

Sharpshooters

Academic Aces

A small, Midwest teacher's college, started around the beginning of this past century has grown to a large state University, supporting a myriad of colleges offering degrees in fields from Anthropology to Zoology. Tests of intellectual acuteness are legendary, as one should expect in such an environment.

One such tilting of the conceptual windmills took place in earlier years in a philosophy department one morning as the students sat for a semester exam. The professor entered the room and walked to the blackboard at the front on which he had earlier written, "Test Essay Question" punctuated by a colon. His students sat mesmerized by the possibilities of academic challenge before them, their minds floating in the nether worlds of metaphysics, awaiting the professor's entrance.

Sweeping into the hall and straight to the front sans hesitation the professor grasped a piece of chalk from the sideboard and finished off the test query with one word, "Why?" Returning the chalk to its' niche, he brushed his hands free of the chalk dust and retreated to his desk to recline with a book and an apple. From the class, almost immediately upon the prof's immersion in his volume, a young student arose and approached the teacher's desk, placing a paper at the corner before turning and exiting with no further ado.

When the test scores were posted a few days later, the class was amazed to discover the young man had received the highest honors. An 'A' had been proscribed by his name. Knowing the professor's stringent grading habits, in particular on essay questions, a number of classmates sought out the teacher to discover the student's reason for his audacity and what answer had been turned in to garner the top grade.

Understanding the consternation of the students the professor drew the test in question from a stack in a drawer and placing it on his desk, stood and walked from the room.

To the foundational question, "Why," which sits as a cornerstone of philosophy, the student had replied with his own philosophical reconnaissance of two words. "Why not?"

Wars of Words

It was a military training class in religion. However, this was a command function at which attendance was mandatory. The theme was the future of this world. Only those few assigned duty elsewhere were absent, along with the usual handful reported to sick call, and the ever vigilant walking point that had seen the class coming and finagled their way out with whatever trumped up duties they could scramble to devise.

Present were most of the many hundreds representing the administration company for which the class was being held. Filling row upon row of steel folding chairs were all those bestowed with the honor of participating, and that included in the back of the hall the hustlers and loafers that ordinarily would have opted out with some slick maneuver of their own making. Their attendance dictated by some with boredom at dodging the game. And with others corralled by hangovers severe enough to care no longer. For whatever reason, all present were in for a morning of religious instruction, Army style, scheduled as 'The Chaplain's Hour.'

Primary focus this morning would be on prophecies of the end times as they might be related to 'military thinking.' Amusement invariably arose at the suggestion of anything orderly being linked with the military, especially in the realms of intellectuality. Many attendees would have, if interviewed, hastened to demand such hyperbole was a contradiction in terms.

Of course there was no mention of the Bible, or for that matter any connection with God. This was the United States Army. Religion had to be parceled out in diplomatic terms. And anyhow, wasn't even eschatology an opportunity to prime the pump for any approaching separations and consequent mandatory re-enlistment counseling? Disaster and catastrophe were welcome helpmeets to discourage all and sundry from considering the civilian life. As the picture began to form of the events foreseen by futurists of all persuasions, the idea of being 'out there' when the earthquakes, famines, pestilences and horror of horrors, wars would begin to ensue, the wise were comforted that 'in here' at least we had the best machine guns. This detail placed prominently first among the lengthy list of advantages to making the Army one's career.

As the stuffy hall filled with silence, and then the smell of fear began to invade the senses, soldiers began to steal glances to see who was buying and who wasn't. Deep in the back a number of the men, a few short-timers among them, turned to nervously look toward one bored Private who seemed half asleep, or hung over, as the warnings droned on without abatement.

Recently reduced in rank just in view of a scheduled promotion, the Private's attendance was a surprise to most. Even the noncoms were chuckling with mild wonder as the 'Most Unlikely Candidate' for religion had filed into the gathering. His position and power had not visibly waned after his court martial. He'd even been allowed to enlist a clerk from the Personnel Services Division to be assigned as his driver. Thus, the Private had attained to the solitary plateau of being the lowest ranking member of the U.S. Army with his own personal chauffer. Even this morning he might have opted out for any number of writing assignments to forego this command assembly. So what was his interest here? You think a guy like the Private and Religion...do you?

As the starkness of the prophecies continued to darken and intensify the speaker began to grow confident in his place and started hollering out in cadence challenges to the truly captive throng. "Anybody care to guess what we're talking about?" he'd called out. "Have any idea what's coming in the future?"

Many of the men were cut off from news sources and stateside TV and radio. Army News was so completely managed, confectioned and processed that it was difficult to know when the speaker was reporting actual events and where he was proclaiming dictated command spin.

Time tumbled backwards in the Private's musings to a winter morning that seemed like eons past. Was it another lifetime? Had it really happened or was it childhood imagination. Memories of the wet shoe squishing and the clammy cold of the sock made the Private smile in spite of himself. No, it had been real enough. The moon had been hanging up there as small as a dime. The chilling discovery he'd made of the locked door of the Sacristy hadn't faded with the years either. And then the race he'd run all the way home. And his childhood chum had remembered the route, too, years later when they'd reminisced about the old days.

"Well, anybody got any bright ideas?" The speaker's gnawing dig broke through the soldier's reverie. "The tribulation," the soldier's call came loud and cold and clear, yet surprisingly bored and disdainful as it broke through the speaker's rhetorical posturing like a clap of thunder in a spring shower.

Necks craned as laughter broke through the silenced crowd in waves of relief. The tension was gone from the hall. It was Saturday morning and just about 10 minutes left in the hour. In fact it was more like eight minutes, maybe even seven now. The speaker had lost his momentum and with it the audience. The remaining moments would be an agonizing scramble to attempt to conclude with at least a semblance of dignity.

Staring from his platform, gazing toward the back of the room where the call had emanated the speaker made one last stab at a retrenchment to order. "Sharpshooters," he announced, nodding to the crowd, "You're always going to find sharpshooters in every crowd."

"Boy, that was great," one of the newly arrived enlisted men marveled as the class ended and the hall began to empty. "That guy was crazy, wasn't he?" he shot at the Private, while chuckling at the deemed idiocy of the speaker's remarks. Others slowed to get the Private's take. "You were kidding, right?" the recent arrival overseas continued, becoming unsure of his ground as the short timer Private continued staring at him. "No, son," the 1st Sergeant clapped the young troop on the shoulder from behind while the Private continued to stand in silent circumspection. "He was serious. The laughter was because the Private was not joking."

Valiant For Truth

Seriousness was not a quality of the hippie movement. At least the outward appearance proffered the 'cool' of the movement to any that cared to observe. "Keep on truckin'," was the motto, and 'mello' was the mood of choice. But truth continued to resurge as the reality most sought after. Moderation always seemed to arise as the 'way.' So he was amazed to say the least when he got her letter. She wrote that she had 'found' Jesus. At least she had found someone who had found Jesus. "And, he's just like you," she reported.

There had been talk that some in the movement, as intentionally disorganized as it was recognized to be, were somehow getting into Jesus. Involvement in drugs and eastern religions were not only common practices among hippies, but natural progressions expected from the constant search for truth. But the idea of drugs leading to Jesus didn't quite fit.

She never really made a connection. She just said she'd met some guy and he had introduced her to the idea of Jesus. He wrote a scathing letter back explaining that people involved in drugs and the hippie lifestyle couldn't possibly know anything about Jesus. He was gratified when she wrote back that she had broken off the relationship to join up with a guy that was into astrology. That somehow made more sense.

Still, he had to wonder about this 'Jesus' thing. There had been something about it when he was younger but that was in another life. It seemed that long ago. Would it be possible to know Jesus personally? Why was that such an intriguing idea to him? What was it about Jesus?

Once again he realized even though you may ask the right question or give the right answer you still might not be anywhere. All was vanity. Wherever he had heard or read that, it was certainly true.

Once in his past he had written, "As there is time for this place, may there always be place for this time." And when he was younger he had believed in Jesus. He thought that he believed in Jesus now. But what made him think he knew who knew Jesus and who didn't? And if he did know Jesus, why did Jesus seem so far away?

He remembered the story of the philosophy student at the college in his hometown university. That had been a neat trick. A quick answer had won the day. It became his model. He had even pulled it off a few times himself. Like that morning in the Army what seemed now like eons ago. But he'd made that remark because he believed that was exactly what the Chaplain had been talking about. Even so, the man had not been able to confirm the point of his own lecture. And, now, the soldier-journalist-actor-hippie was not so sure he himself could believe any of it anymore. The officer had left the challenge unmet for some unknown reason. Or could it be the officer had in fact been agreeing that the futurist observations were alluding to the Tribulation?

Without adornment, a sharpshooter is one who bulls-eye's the target. Had the joke been on the Private and the assembly of soldiers? Perhaps the Chaplain had made his point in spades and had won the last laugh. Yet who would admit that they were talking about the end of the world coming anyway? Only 'whackos' did stuff like that. Smart, intelligent, educated people always left room to navigate.

Then one day, when more years had passed, the hippie found himself reading aloud from the Holy Bible. He had been a voracious reader from early in his childhood. The list of titles he'd traversed was prodigious for breadth of topic as well as depth of detailed analysis of subject. He would expose that education in almost any conversation, often even inadvertently. So it came as a cold shock to realize he'd never read the Bible. And embarrassingly, it was made up of books, of which he had read not a single volume in its' entirety. Striving for optimum efficiency while redressing this literary over-sight, he began to read the King James Version aloud. His effort was two-fold. First he could practice speaking writ formed in the day and language of Shakespeare, and secondly he could gather simultane-ously the jewels embedded in this work of renown and wisdom. He did just fine until the words he was reading began to echo as screams in his ears.

He was then forced to stop because the words were resounding with such force in his own hearing that he had to break and discover the meaning of this happening. He shared with a friend that he had put the book away because he realized it was alive. That book was trying to tell him, yes, and not he alone, but the world...it was trying to tell the world a message. It was trying, no, not just him, but it was trying to contact the world with a specific purpose. He just didn't know what that message could be. So disconcerting was the experience he put the Bible aside to await future direction. He knew as he did so, not from where or whom or what quarter that revelation would arrive.

A few weeks, a month or so perhaps, following that jarring a book was brought to his attention that had only been in the market-place a few years. Everything was in the title: *The Late Great Planet Earth*.[66] The statement was a cross between show business and newspaper journalism. One profession he'd come out of and the other he was now plying as his trade.

And in this document the author was confirming his own asser-tions with the Bible. Or was the Bible giving the author the confir-mations for his own search? Whichever the case, there was not only a lack of avoidance of point, the point was being driven home with the confidence of a Captain at the helm of a hurricane tossed fishing boat, bobbing like a cork in the Atlantic.

Twenty-fours later the 'any man' was kneeling on a living room floor asking Jesus to come into his heart and save him so that he could know for certain that he was going to live forever. A sharp-shooter was biting the dust.

I John 5:13 [67] was the verse that really got him. "These things I have written to you who believe in the name of the Son of God, that you may know you have eternal life, and that you may continue to believe in the name of the Son of God."

There it was in black and white. No room for doubt or even speculation. Those who believed were instructed to know. And he, who prided himself on knowing or being able to find the answer if he didn't, knew for certain that he did not know for certain if he had eternal life.

As he began to devour the Bible the memories of that cold winter morning, so distant in the past, began to return. And the memory that there was time for now was developing into the understanding that now was the time for the beginning of 'here ever after.' And now knowing there is a hereafter, he began to realize that for many 'now' was swiftly becoming 'too late.'

CHAPTER VIII

Why We Should Then Go

'C'elebrity' captures the top spot in today's social whirl. The combination of films and television has unintentionally yet exponentially fragmented society's proceedings. Outside the influence of participation of even the least of the members of this inner circle of humanity the luster of any celebration is dulled if not ignored completely.

Before he gained even wider recognition, TV's Regis Philbin described his disappointment at eating at a restaurant in Hollywood famed for its' status as a hangout of the 'Stars.' "I was the biggest star there," he exasperated one morning on his talk show with Kathy Lee Gifford before she split for new pastures. "Me, the biggest star," he laughed in mock self-deprecation.

So powerfully had this modern phenomenon developed in the Twentieth Century that by the 50's movie stars were successfully out-leveraging Washington bureaucrats handily. A story comes to mind of a function of political leaders one evening in D.C. A line was formed to receive the public. As the senators were greeting their constituents, John Wayne entered a doorway across the floor of the hall being used. The senators en masse abandoned the voters to themselves and rushed across the floor to meet the Duke. And within their actions were displayed the disintegration of the paradigm of the democratic vote.

Consequently perhaps one of the most socially profound testimonies to be recorded in recent years concerning the salvation experience of someone coming to accept Jesus as their Lord and Savior would have to be the startling confession of faith made by Hollywood superstar Jane Fonda.

She had already reached fame when future spouse Ted Turner helmed *Courageous* to a sparkling 4-0 shut out over *Australia* to retain the 1977 America's Cup. No mystery that he arrived at the awards banquet three sheets to the wind! Fonda has developed over the years an image in the world at large of 'ultra cool.' She does of course hale from the Silver Screen Fonda clan. Her brother Peter deeply impacted society with *Easy Rider*, a film that continues to influence many writers, directors and actors nearly four decades out. Father and revered film legend, the late Henry Fonda, doffed his integrity compelling the fans worldwide to return time and again to movie houses to admire his creations of character after character embued with sterling truthfulness. It is no surprise Jane honed her many abilities to become a renowned actress.

An early stint as a political activist surprised many at the seriousness of this Hollywood child whose anti-war stance was underlined by trips to North Viet Nam to pose with America's enemy. In an age of increasingly forgiving attitudes for any and all manner of transgressions, reminders of her youth occasionally return to trouble her. Even though the conflict 'become a War' ended in 1975.

Bringing an air of respectability to many films that would otherwise have been relegated as B-grade fanciful reaches, Fonda ably portrayed a news reporter in 'China Syndrome.' The plot has her discover a government agency's cover up at a nuclear power plant. The film came chillingly close to reality within days of premiere when the meltdown at Three Mile Island occurred. So close to the revelation of truth, this happening was neatly and hastily passed over by the powers that be in the media and Show Biz. Perhaps a case of 'too close for comfort.' Much of the media and most in Hollywood predictably reverted to the schlock they produce ad nauseam, incapable of dealing with life when it explodes in their presence. Following a few brief notices at the amazing coincidence of art preceding life, the film was ignored and let drift into the shadows.

Her marriage to Turner on the contrary was thought news so worthy that shots of the two of them at his team's World Series games were deemed notable. Though little was said of Mr. T's snoring through the midst of one contest.

Mercifully, her profession of Christianity has not suffered the media assault other celebrities have had to endure, such as Mr. Bob Dylan, persuading all but the most jaded that those in the media may have some sensibilities after all, though rarely exercised.

Curiously, a televised interview of La Fonda by Barbara Walters,[68] who has never been known to miss a glaring opportunity to parse major moves of any kind made by the glitterati, ensconced the meeting in the conspicuous with a total pass of this eternal step. Entire lives have been spent striving to satisfy the holy compunction to tell the world of this experience of being saved. And a public profession of faith in Jesus by such a social worthy would also be thought pronouncement needful of notation. Doubly, conversation to be wafted to the millions of viewers imparts the expectation that monumental moments, more so of eternal import, be acknowledged. Yet, this divinely historical jot was somehow bypassed by Ms. Walters, a broadcast journalist who has had the temerity, dare one suggest *chutzpah*, to face off the toughest and also most delicate situations with admirable poise. Admittedly, there were not eternal manifestations in other publicized conversations to be weighed. Even still many in the glare of show business continue to mystify the public in their displays of perceptual relevance.

Beyond that the proclamation of such a high profile subject has excited many in the Body of Messiah to believe once again that not only all are within reach, but that even those seemingly most disenfranchised are possible to be claimed for Jesus, and all attempts are indeed worth the cross.

In that vein, an even greater stir followed the reports in the press a couple decades back of Dylan's conversion experience. But the media carnival that flowered following his efforts to maintain equilibrium left him few choices for any continuing peace. It should not be left unsaid that his Jewishness added a spiritual depth all its' own to the fervor of attention. Yet his then consequential return to the Judaism of his youth can now, in the light of the growing Messianic movement, cause one to wonder at the possible blossoming of prophetical fulfillments beyond the know of mere mortals.

So then also what finally develops from Fonda's walk with the Lord will be intriguing. Her spiritual journey brings to mind that of other actors, actresses and assorted luminaries through the centuries.

Perhaps the most notable theatrical personage to be associated with the Gospel would be William Shakespeare himself. It has been suggested that Shakespeare quoted directly from Scripture over 500 times in his writings. Certainly the influence of Scripture could hardly have been ignored by the young playwright with the translation of the King James Version of the Bible in the works coinciding with his own literary strivings. In fact the publishing date of the first edition of the KJV and Hamlet coincide at 1608.

The Bard's final thoughts were legalized in his will to his family and friends. Amidst his departing assurances, this testimony to his Lord, "I commend my soul into the hands of God my Creator, hoping and assuredly believing through the only merits of Jesus Christ my Savior to be made partaker of Life Everlasting." [69]

This is not to suggest that anyone and everyone who has named the name of Jesus is a Christian. But certainly, that would allow the consideration of a start at the very minimum. Jesus did say, "Therefore whoever confesses Me before men, him I will also confess before My Father who is in heaven." (Matt. 10:32-33) [70]

One would think that such highlights of evangelistic outreach would be the very stuff of encouragement to be found to fuel the ardor of missionaries and their agencies. And hopefully, that these spiritual milestones would ignite a seeking of how close the world is to Jesus' Return. If these remarkable conversions at this late day highlight the approach of His stepping onto the Mount of Olives, then how much closer is our calling out which is set seven years prior to His return? It would also seem even natural that missionaries would be the very people with the sharpest focus on this coming Blessed Event. Yet the shock is to discover that many serving Him most ardently at this moment are the very ones least prepared for this imminent prophetical riptide.

As life would have it, this writer came into contact with a woman working with an international evangelistic group. Believing the heart of this missionary was for the lost souls of humanity, it was natural to attempt to encourage such a dedicated servant of the Lord with a reminder to be looking up.

"Why would God send me out if He was going to rapture me in the next hour," she asked, in scorn and derision, a hearty, mocking laugh lacing her question with the finality of doctrinal assurance? "Why would He send us? Why did God tell me to go?" she emphasized, exposing the absurdity of an imminent evacuation.

Remember. She's the one with the support of an international agency. She's the one with the speaking schedule. She's the one with the commitments.

And then the reality broke upon me. The volatility of the teaching of His Imminence couches within it the immediate threat to the status quo. It's fine to teach that Jesus is going to return. It's even acceptable to say He is coming soon. It would even be allowable to say His return may be very near. But don't start going around saying His Rapture is going to be any moment. Of course His return is not going to be any moment because, as we've noted before, His return is going to follow seven years of hell on earth. But we're looking at the Rapture. No one knows when the Return is going to be. Only that it will follow seven years after the Rapture, at the finish of seven years of prophecy fulfillments. That's not putting a date on the Return, which is placing prophecy in perspective. And, further, Paul didn't put a date on the Rapture either, he said, "...then we who are alive and remain shall be caught up..." Paul wasn't looking to a day; he was looking to a moment. Why did Jesus say, "...do not worry about tomorrow...?"[71] See also, Hebrews 3:13 and especially Hebrews 10:25. Remember, seek and ye shall find. "...as you see the day approaching."[72] Every day is called today. Except of course, tomorrow. And then there is yesterday. But here lies today. To act on His imminent calling up is too threatening to this 'now' we know to be. Notice the phrase, status quo.

This dear, worldly successful missionary was convinced God wouldn't send her out if He were returning any moment. But what if He wasn't returning any moment, but any moment He can call her out? At least He wouldn't call her out without prior notice, she contended. So what is Bible prophecy, chopped liver? It's not anywhere on her schedule. Why, He couldn't. He wouldn't dare even think of such a thing! No, God would tell her if He were going to come back at any moment. He is a God of orderly progression. How is one able to interpret six thousand years of prophetical fulfillment as somehow insufficient or even disorderly notice?

How much time did God give Moses as he approached the burning bush before He commanded Moses to take his shoes off because Moses was standing on Holy Ground?

How much time did Jesus give Lazarus before He shouted for Lazarus to come forth?

How much time is God going to give the world before the Rapture? No one knows is the standard and safe answer. And even the implication that the Rapture could happen at any moment as we live and breathe is deemed fanciful, dangerous and even fanatical. We do not know at the very least how much time God has given the world before the Shout and the Trumpet blast. So far it has been 2,000 years give or take a decade.

Well then, if it's been that long, how much longer might it then be? No one knows the answer to that question either. But have you ever noticed whenever the question is asked, "How short is the time before Jesus returns?" There's scant mention of His calling His Bride away from the earth first. And the reply of any time always carries with it the understanding of now or later but never suggests at any moment.

Another wording is, "How *much longer* do you think it will be before He comes?" Certainly even Scripture provides the query, "How long, O Lord?" For many dozens of pleas are made throughout the *Tanakh* and the *B'rit Chadashah*. Parenthetically, these Hebraic terms for the works more popularly recognized as the Old and New Testaments are fittingly in place when the study involves the restoration of Israel. Even into heaven and unto the very Throne of God the prayer reaches. "And they cried with a loud voice, 'How long, O Lord, holy and true, until You judge and avenge our blood on those who dwell on the earth?'" (Rev. 6:10) [73] Though this call for God's intervention is prophetically set during the Tribulation following the Rapture, still, the more accurate concern remains unknown. How *short*, O Lord, is our time? We may only acknowledge with Job, "My days are swifter than a weaver's shuttle." (Job 7:6) [74] We too must submit with the Psalmist that our times are in His hands. Yet if our days are so fleeting, how abrupt shall be His call to come up yonder?

Some have suggested Jesus' Return would transpire in their lifetime. Others have even subscribed to a specific day, hour and year. The predictions have all been wrong. Gives the heart a safe, warm, fuzzy feeling of assurance, doesn't it? All things remain as they have been, *ergo*, the conclusion goes, if all predictions have missed their day then His Return is either way off in the future or even perhaps not at all.

But then the pendulum begins to swing back. Peter's warning suddenly gains new immediacy. "Knowing this first: that scoffers will come in the last days, walking according to their own lusts, and saying, "Where is the promise of His coming? For since the fathers fell asleep, all things continue as they were from the beginning of creation." (II Peter 3:3) [75] Two more specifics should be marked here. It is in the last days that the ridicule of His Return shall become open derision. And familiarity with His word of creation shall become so commonplace as to foster the judgment of contempt. To give an example, have you ever seen the devastation of disorder in a Bible bookstore the day after Christmas?

The 11/100's of a second transition time is not a lot to work with. Yet that is the sum total of the turn around time relegated to the Rapture. Instead of the imminent return being a doctrine that discourages missionary endeavors, it should, as used by Paul, be the very thing of encouragement to all out effort. Paul would not have us to be ignorant.

"Why should we even go?" the missionary had asked incredulously. Is that a good point or not? Would you invest in a mission outreach where no church had ever been? What about where there would be no visible increase for your effort? Who's going to go out to the field and work at the end of the day, even if someone is foolish enough to hire them? Who would volunteer for a mission outreach by paying with a couple planks and a few old, rusty nails? A person could lose their shirt. A guy could even lose his life if he wasn't careful. These things have to be checked out. Forgive the lapse into sarcasm. Perhaps the better response would be to ask, why then are you going?

A friend asked for a good book to buy. It was suggested that she consider a work that dealt with prophecy. "It will take you years of study to get through this book," she was warned. "And, of course, you may not have time to finish it anyway," she was encouraged.

And anyone that might be struggling with adjusting to using Hebrew words to describe the concepts of God; imagine their shock upon meeting the King of Israel. And it all will be finalized in 11/100's of a second. At least the prophecy of the Rapture shall be finalized in the twinkling of an eye. The actual restoration of Israel shall happen seven years following the twinkle give or take a smile!

CHAPTER IX

He Will Make A Short Work

An intriguing passage looms out of Romans 9, Paul's gaze deepening into the increase and riches of God's mercies toward His first love, Israel.

"For He will finish the work and cut it short in righteousness, because the Lord will make a short work upon the earth." (Romans 9:28.)[76]

George Gershwin, like many men before him and after, sought well into his adult life for the approbation of his father. Gershwin's involvement with show business and work as a musician only lessened his opportunity to gain his father's approval for his life. The elder Gershwin did not deem as worthy the craft of writing songs even for Broadway musicals.

Still after George began to gain respect and popularity as a composer in his chosen profession, it was difficult to get Gershwin senior to encourage his pursuit. Money and fame grew in disproportionate measure to the decreasing interest offered by his dad for his burgeoning success.

Then came the evening of the debut of what would become George's signature composition, "Rhapsody in Blue." Hoping against odds that this work would finally win him paternal respect, Gershwin invited his father to the concert. He made certain a box downstage left front was reserved. His father would be given the optimum vantage of perspective. Gershwin senior would witness the performance of what was to become honored by many as America's premier jazz composition.

Audience response was overwhelming, with electric curtain call following curtain call demanded of the composer. And the richness and longevity of the number would ensure waves of adulation to unfold into future decade after decade.

But Gershwin's attention that evening returned again and again through the accolades to the first box down stage left, to the figure of a man, seated, and unmindful of the applause, who could be seen studying the face of an opened pocket watch.

Backstage, George met his father eagerly awaiting the words he'd labored so diligently over the years to receive. "Not bad," his father commended, again studying his timepiece. "It was over seven minutes long. You're getting better."

Length of time as a measurement in significance renders its' own distinct though not always accurate proportion to everything in our world. Size in any realm can also be misleading. Napoleon's conquests are often set against his diminutive stature. His lack of height is often outlined before listing his accomplishments, as if to suggest wonder that a small man could do great things. Conversely, Sam Houston was six foot six inches tall. That is rarely noted, and even ignored by historians, again suggesting accomplishments by large men to be inferred as expected when accomplished.

Great works in literature are assumed to be extensive. "Gone With The Wind," and "War and Peace," come to mind, if merely for their sheer volume. Dramatists emphasize the greatness of a work by nothing more than '…it's full length,' redundantly explaining they are referencing a four-act play. Occasionally in history writing has been published that quantum leaped the rules of order. Most often came the tomes of vast verbiage with no meaning. Or sometimes insanity expressed in such dark form that it was misinterpreted as simply poorly written thought, or yet worse, as esoterically inspired brilliance. *Mein Kampf*, screams to be first in this genre, and may win the prize.

In this vein follow the volumes of the artists that are published and defended for their sheer size, i.e., The Works of ...etc. Surely, with all of this paper and effort, and such an abundance of phrase, especially if it is unfathomable, we must be in the presence of genius.

Stellar contributions to history, literary and otherwise, offer clarity and impact, size aside. Lincoln's "Gettysburg Address," is unavoidable in all of literature for its' breathtaking insight encased in sterling and historically poetic brevity. Jesus' lack of response before Pilate astounds with its' ringing absence of defense, though our Lord was in fact also fulfilling prophecy. (see Isaiah 53:7)[77] The invention of the wheel must be noted, though the salutations must remain sans address. George Washington Carver's hundreds of myriad discoveries through the lowly peanut conflict the mind with humility.

Yet size and volume also have their place. *The Complete Works of William Shakespeare* as a title, bears easily the weight of proclamation. Sir Edmund Hillary and Tenzing Norkay on Everest's summit lift the heart to noble conquest. In permutation, though the disaster of the Titanic has done much to enhance the fame of that vessel, logic escapes as to why such a maritime disaster should be so fondly remembered.

And so we appreciate archaeology on through to zoology in all historic aspects and realms. And especially enjoy the new perspectives flung in lightning speed across the Internet, error atop fact atop speculation, enticingly beckoning to be disentangled as knowledge now purportedly doubles every four months. Of course what stands for knowledge today is exquisitely demonstrated by example in the plethora of fast food chains, disconnected islands offering overpriced portions of neither quickness nor sustenance. Hidden throughout the jungle of eateries lies the occasional oasis that must be heralded for its' heroic continuance in the face of all opposition.

Enchantment with vanity only grows however, and now we sit, this truly at the beginning of the new millennium by some calculators, having suffered through a year's false start we are told, once again breathlessly focused on the future and what it shall bring.

After all, all things continue as they were, do they not, and we know that there is really nothing to know except that things will go on ad infinitum. Lives are being lived. Wars are being won and lost. New records break with tiresome speed. Gains made. Losses absorbed.

And then we read, "For He will finish the work and cut it short in righteousness, because the Lord will make a short work upon the earth."

Well! But what of Gibbon's *Decline and Fall of the Roman Empire*, one might ask? What of all the marvelous new mega dams in China? They'll be finished in a few more years, or decades, many of them. Have you seen the pictures? 'Impressive' doesn't sketch the outline.

Notice Paul states the Lord will finish the work and cut it short in righteousness, and then explains that the emphasis needs be on the why of the thing. Why? Because the Lord will make a short work upon the earth; we can then expect history to wrap quickly when God has completed His plan. Just one indication that God is coming to the end of his 'to do' list is His prophecies that deal with His returning Israel to their land. Where were you in 1948? The primary reference book to check on this last statement is called The Holy Bible. The number of verses involved is significant. Great is the listing of books available in libraries and the market place on this subject. The media is replete with television, radio, newspapers and articles focusing on this specific area of study.

But we already understand the Rapture is predicted as an imminent event that demands no prerequisite event. And no finish in fact is involved in that prophecy either. 'Things' shall keep on keeping on. A minor adjustment is all that God will be making. His Bride is to be escorted away from the trials that shall then come upon the earth. For those ready for His shout, you may be encouraged to continue preparing for the Wedding feast! More of that if time permits.

And here we have a prophecy of the true ending of what we understand to be history that God merely considers a 'work.' And lo and behold, it is God who is doing the making! He's been in charge all along. He's had a plan and work apportioned from before the beginning. In fact, before the foundation of the world, God already had a plan.[78] And in this passage He is described as finishing the work and cutting it short, because He wants to make it a brief work. There is evidently something beyond the finish of this world that God is otherwise occupied with.

And when the time comes to finish this work, He is going to cut it short! Jesus told the apostles that no man knows the times or season in which He will restore the "...kingdom to Israel." (Acts 1:6c[79]) A gargantuan perspective leaps from the quotation as we are confronted by the preposition 'to.' Had the text read 'of' we would not have been halted in our way. That would have lent itself to the understanding of one amongst many. But the predictive 'to' at the very least outlines 'first among many' and well merits 'only' which gains support through the God of the Sh'ma, and Jesus' description of Heaven as a kingdom. And, certainly, there are no promises throughout Scripture that ensure an eternal place for any kingdom other than Israel.

Invariably when this passage from Acts is referenced it is concerning the end of the world. The question posed, however, looks to the restoration of the kingdom to Israel. Who is looking for that? A popular interpretation has been that the Church is Israel in the New Covenant. But Jesus had said, Matt. 16:18,[80] He would build His Church and the gates of hell would not prevail against it. And then in the opening of Acts He acknowledges that Israel shall be restored. Two separate entities by His view. And, of course, for clarity's purpose it must be recorded their question is one of restoration not of building. So it would be Israel which is looking for its' rebirth. The Church on the other hand is being built.

But before Israel can be restored the world must go through the time of Jacob's trouble. And Jacob's trouble cannot begin, Israel's present trials acknowledged, before the Church is kept from those end-time trials that shall come upon all the earth.

How much time then have we been promised before the Rapture? None. Paul was expecting the Rapture at any moment during his day. He said, "...then, we who are alive..."[81] leaving no doubt that he expected the event at any moment.

Only the happening itself is made known. And the completion of this promise is not the length of a seven-minute composition that has entertained generations. Nor is it the scant moment taken to offer a penitent plea that touches the throne of God. The enactment of this prophecy shall encompass 11/100's of a second start to finish. People shall witness the first part of a greater movement of prophecy God is constructing. And this shall only begin His promise to cut short that which we call History. This supernatural declension of the human race called the Rapture shall be the shortest sermon ever. And it shall encompass the twinkling of an eye. Quicker than you can think 'Amen.'

CHAPTER X

When Now Becomes
Almost Too Late

D r. J. Vernon McGee[82] loved to unwind after his Sunday
evening service by curling up in bed with a good mystery
novel. The marvelous preacher, who has become known over the
past many decades to multiplied millions of radio listeners across
the earth, even continuing to shepherd Christians with his recorded
programs after he joined the Lord a decade or so back, admitted one
eccentricity.

Reading mystery novels was an extremely relaxing form of
recreation to him. And after a busy Sunday of ministering the Word,
he looked forward to this pastime. But he confessed that he knew he
would fall asleep before he had finished a few chapters of the book.
And so his practice became to turn to the last page as he began each
book to discover who had committed the crime. This way he could
fall asleep contentedly, knowing how the story was going to turn
out.

He also often used this practice as an illustration of sound
Christian living. He would encourage those worried about the

outcome of life to turn to the final chapter of the Bible that describes the new heaven and the new earth with Jesus firmly in control of our eternal future.[83]

These prophecies are frequently alluded to as Christian 'pie in the sky' hopes and dreams…a kind of crutch mentality for coping with life. From the world's point of view anyone who takes these promises literally is considered to be at the very best, just a tad thick in the head.

How unrealistic is a future hope? One might ask the same question for what is called the 'present.' It is striking how disoriented the public is in the main when they are asked to position themselves in time and space.

In today's high-tech society there is a distinct lack of recognition that life has passed from the casual to the exact. 'Anytime' is no longer an acceptable answer to the question of when an event can take place. Also, though you may understand what 'anytime' infers, you still are unable to communicate that knowledge into the system except where the system has been programmed to receive such. Systems are incapable of receiving general instructions such as, "They always know where to look." And "you know what I mean," is not applicable simply because the phrase is not recognizable unless written into the program. 'You understood,' is not a part of the grammar in a program.

A college student recently was studying the topic of the 'Historical Jesus,' when he was challenged with the prospect of meeting personally, for himself, the real Jesus. Striving to get some perspective on this Person that has so dominated history with His life, death and resurrection, the student was missing the point of Jesus' coming in the first place. One cannot schedule an appointment for 'Today from 7 a.m. to 5 p.m.' when it is already mid-morning. A request of 'anytime,' which is an unrecognizable description to a computer program, also won't compute. The young man is seeking to know the past of the One who wants to meet him here and now in the student's own present reality. Like the computer program, the student is simply not receiving the message being offered to him.

For those laboring in a society of scholars that deem man's

beginning as descending from the apes, primates then being human-ity's closest relatives, amusement passes to wonder that so many truly are unclear of what 'origin' actually means.

Two of the questions that immediately arise out of these realiza-tions are, where did I come from? And, where am I going? The inner-relation of these two themes with each other and the topic at hand is hopefully apparent and at least intended. This focus brings us full circle to the consideration of the impending Rapture. If the evacuation of the Bride truly takes place before the Tribulation, then that 'now' that follows shall have become almost 'too late.'

However, if a person is incapable of confirming his history, he would be hard pressed to know his future, which certainly says something for the elderly Statesman who has spent his career delv-ing into the past. But if one ignores all of the parameters of time he then becomes ill prepared to step into the future.

Especially how could he identify 'when now becomes almost too late?' And what response could he offer when that point of instantaneous change befalls the world at the enactment of the Bride's exit at the Lord's command. Certainly, one immediate ques-tion arising from this scenario might be, how much time does he then have?

It has already been seen that you cannot be guaranteed 11/100's of a second. Nor can even the twinkling of an eye be assured. Because, we truthfully can only be assured of the moment in which we find ourselves. Anything beyond this 'now' we inhabit can only be viewed as pure speculation.

And if now is all we possess, as quickly as we are moving through this day and age, we are constantly becoming too late. For the next moment is always too late for the now we inhabit. And the Bible warns there is a 'now' coming which shall be irreversible. And that certainly would be when now definitely becomes too late.

CHAPTER XI

The Rapture

My breath was stopped. A horrendous sound from outside the earth was forcing my vision upward toward the heavens. Lack of breath accentuated my attention riveted to the skies as they separated by elements against a sound of winds ten thousand times ten thousand overwhelming with awe as light broke through the scattered pieces of disintegrating sky and the Holy Spirit whispered in my heart, "It's the Rapture, Terry, don't be afraid."

The mind moved at a rate eclipsing any speed ever described by man, all the while capturing every collapse of the realities of this now, sensing the body hurtling upwards through the infinite openings of space itself, defying all intellectual strivings for human comprehension. This was it! Even as I struggled to identify the happenings, bodies all around the sky vaulted upwards.

Mixed images forced their way upon my meager perception as I recognized a fellow employee, Mark. And there was Pat, the supervisor, focused on the journey upward, her eyes wide with shock.

School children lined up neatly with men all around, guiding them into lines as they came from the earth. And we in our casual clothes, Mark, Pat and I ushered into a room filled with people in formal attire sitting in choirs singing hymns of praise. Their startled, displeasured grimaces at our arrival in casual clothes gave way to they're returning to the songs in adulation to the Lord.

And then it was pitch black and I was lying in my bed panting audibly, still in shock myself, captivated yet by the roar of a mighty rushing wind. Dogs in the distance began to bark, yard by yard, they awoke, the yelps growing louder and more intense as the object of their intentions drew closer. Rising from bed I parted the blinds and peered out into the backyard and beyond to the alley. A lone figure was scurrying through the night unmindful of the hostile growls of canines. He had long black hair against his black shirt and trousers. An alien himself, he was ever so natural in his habitat of the dark.

Crawling back under the covers, I lay there listening to the baying of the dogs die away only to realize the rush of the wind was still a cacophony in my ears. Twenty more minutes passed before the silence finally returned, and I lay still, fully awake. "Lord," I called in my heart, "What was it?" Slowly, through the remainder of the night He opened different parts of the vision.

The Rapture would be that powerful and more. None, even those looking for it would be prepared for the immensity of it all. No amount of preparation would allow for the shock of release of instantaneous power that is coming in this event. No meditation or study will adequately arrange the mind for what is to come. Only the immediate care of He Who comes alongside, the Paraclete, the *Ruach HaKodesh*, the Comforter, the Holy Spirit will avail the sojourner of the fortitude to withstand this eternal and awesome onslaught of change known as the Rapture.

Angels will be dispatched especially to bring the children that shall be snatched away. For them it will be like an early release from school for eternity. Their agile imaginations will be far more adaptable to the transition than adults and they will be comforted.

And what of those in the formal attire? Many believers have not accepted the deeper measures of the doctrine of the Rapture and so their minds can grasp even less of the reality of this Blessed Hope than the few that are ready, listening and watching. And so their imaginations stop them at the formal boundaries of their intellects.

There simply is no way for them to understand what is coming and so their formalized perceptions will be shattered instantaneously.

After waking my wife and describing the dream, there in the early hours of the new day, it was she who readily recognized the person of the Holy Spirit, the mighty rushing wind. I was shocked to realize the eternal power to be unleashed from that phrase that in its' reality went unrecognized by me, though the familiarity of the phrase from Acts is completely immediate to my knowledge. It was so far beyond what it reads to be.

Only days had passed since the dream. Yet, the sound had not gone from my memory. Even the echoes of roaring remain awesome to the point of verging on overwhelming, immobilizing fear. All this mesmerizing dream from beginning a book a few months before about that moment in time, 11/100's of a second, which shall transform the earth as no other previous event in history save the Resurrection. Yet He admonished, "Don't be afraid."

Amazingly, on a website fitted to witness to the world of the need for individual salvation, one man wrote a stinging rebuke to help correct those who have been led astray into the misguided perception that Jesus is actually going to return.

Following several paragraphs of interpreting scriptures, that to his carnal mind proved the inaccuracy and error of Christian teaching, the unbeliever finished his tirade with a knowing statement for emphasis. "Jesus will not ever return."

What a devastating shock to this man will be the Rapture! And then, seven years later, if the man lives through the Tribulation, how ashamed he will be to meet Jesus Himself!

Right now, this man is convinced of his understanding. And he is with the majority of those that walk this earth, and that number sadly includes many with the name of Christian. By their estimation either the Bible is wrong, or the interpretation is in error, or both. At least the half of it that deals with Jesus, the Resurrection, the Rapture and Return they mark as false. And if this man is so convinced, with so many others that are equally persuaded that these teachings are then false, certainly, how could any of these things be true? Search the Scriptures.

When the passage from II Peter 3[84] was referenced, he suggested the effort was being made to change the subject. Goodness. How much plainer can communication get? "Where is the promise of His coming?" Is that question so removed from the statement, "Jesus will not ever return.?"

"Therefore, beloved, looking forward to these things, be diligent to be found by Him in peace, without spot and blameless." (II Peter 3:14) [85]

Comfort one another with these words.

EPILOGUE

After Now Comes Forever

I n the final chapter of the book of Revelation, in verse six, the angel of the Lord tells John the Apostle and the reader, "These words are faithful and true."[86] Then they are informed that, "...the Lord God of the holy prophets sent His angel to show His servants the things which must shortly take place."

Three times in the rest of this chapter Jesus Himself emphasizes, "Behold, I am coming quickly!" If He is coming quickly, and this points to His return to the earth, then how much closer must be the Rapture? And then the angel emphasizes to John in verse 10, "Do not seal the words of the prophecy of this book, for the time is at hand." The Lord wants this message to be proclaimed.

A desire of the writer of this study has been to bring to bear, if even in the slightest fashion, the doctrine of the imminent Rapture of the Church, a teaching that is intended to embolden all believers to focus on our Blessed Hope, the impending elopement of the Bride of HaMashiach. Underlining this marvelous truth is the encouragement that can fuel all the mission endeavors that shall ever be inspired.

In verse six we have been instructed by the angel of the Lord that Jesus' return is at hand. That it must, '…shortly take place…' is not referring to the Rapture, but rather the prophecy is to His stepping onto the Mount of Olives to end the Tribulation. Various troubles around the earth even today confirm to many world watchers as well as surveyors of God's Word that drastic change must occur or the end of the world is upon us.

It has been chronicled that Jacques Cousteau, renowned sea explorer, on one of that great adventurer's last journeys before his death, traveled to the Amazon. On that journey, questioned on his view of the future for the earth, it was reported Cousteau could not be hopeful.

To participate in the Rapture one must accept Jesus as Messiah, we are told in the Thessalonian passage quoted in this study. It is for believers only. The exclusiveness could not be more emphatic.

Each of us must meet the Lord Jesus when and where He calls us. He is searching for each of us through the Holy Spirit working through a multitude of believers in vast fields of labor, fields that Jesus described as even in His day, "…already white unto harvest." (John 4:35) [87] Jesus also noted that, "…the harvest is the end of the age." (Matt. 13:39) [88]

Also a hope is to be extended to those that may find this book after the Rapture has occurred. *When Now Becomes Too Late*, is a warning against missing that Blessed event. Yet, even then, there shall be time to repent and accept the Lord Jesus. The penalty on earth in those days for believing in Jesus shall be death if the believer is captured by the powers that then shall briefly reign. But it shall be death unto life eternal. And many shall make that choice and will be exceedingly glad for doing so. For when a person accepts the Lord Jesus, their now becomes forever.

Because the manner of presentation, which includes a number of autobiographical remembrances, may seem out of place in an exposition of Bible prophecy, the writer first of all wishes to impart the reality that the Christian life is a personal experience. Though the admonition in our hectic world is often, "…don't take this personally" this study is written to implore the reader to receive this information first of all as personally addressed. You will or will not personally take part in the Rapture. In addition, the desire is also to expose the reader to the understanding of a three-fold purpose.

Paul notes in Galatians 5:11,[89] "...the offense of the cross," a reality well known to those who follow Jesus. And so the initial offering of this determination is to establish comfort, "...especially to those of the household of faith." (Gal. 6:10) [90] Believers active in the pursuit of His Holy Will are most readily positioned to receive the encouragement the proclamation of the Rapture bestows.

God's Holy Will is seen in Jesus' reply prayer given at the Apostles' request. He answered, "Pray in this manner, 'Our Father, in heaven Hallowed be Your name. Your Kingdom come." (Luke 11:2) [91]

Immediately the reader is catapulted to the horizon of purpose. Life is not merely concerned with what we are about. Life is moreover a preliminary of what is to come.

Understanding the 'twinkling of an eye' is imminent, at any moment as we move and breathe, is electrifyingly awesome to consider for the laborer in the field. Good news from a far country without question. Moreover, it is the veil of hope that shrouds the believer's path from the glare and heat of this desert passage of incredulity.

Secondly, it is recognized that the Body of Messiah is in need of refreshing for these final challenging moments of spiritual warfare that have become so distressingly manifest in our day. That Y'shua may return in this century is of small note to the realist laboring through the daily strife on this mortal coil we move. That He shall shout at any moment, to call out those waiting to meet Him in the air, is the stuff of Gospel songs and praises! That the timing of the inception of that event has been clocked at 11/100's of a second is also a joy unspeakable and full of Glory!

Finally, as Jesus is the Alpha and Omega, the First and the Last, He Who has declared the end from the beginning, so we must understand the end of all things on this earth shall come. Jesus said, "Heaven and Earth shall pass away but My word shall not pass away."[92] Dr. Van Impe believes this teaching refers to a changing over of the earth, a renewal rather than the complete destruction of the old earth. Whatever the process, this world shall not remain as we know it because Jesus said it would not.

In Paul's opening remarks to the Ephesians he focuses in momentarily on the conclusion of these matters in verse 10, "...that in the dispensation of the fullness of the times He might gather together in one all things in Christ, both which are in Heaven and which are on earth...in Him." (Eph 1:10[93])

Once again we are faced with the inevitable finality of life. As a child can be suddenly brought to awareness of the conclusion of this life, so each of us is turned to the ultimate completion of all things as they are in this known sphere of time.

In coming to the decision to form this abbreviated introduction to the doctrine of the Rapture several instantaneous resolves were immediately accepted. First the recognition that to some this teaching shall be a blessing while to others a warning, and still others a curse. It was also obvious that in accepting the prophecy that the Rapture is imminent, that it can happen at any moment, formulates the understanding that all works, including this one at hand, may be interrupted at any point. A tenuous place in which we now find ourselves is the primary problem of such realization for this writer to discover that phrase which will finish the work adequately. If the choice is in fact made available, that will summarize the intention of the body of consideration, which was to strive to focus on the actuality of the moments that we walk through in life. Each of which, however ordinary or extraordinary in its' own extents, is so all consuming in aspect as to drive from the mind not only the continuous, unstoppable forward motion of life, but the unshakable fact that this 'now' we inhabit shall end.

Death, per example, is often so boringly shocking. Surprise. Surprise. We never knew it was going to happen to this one or that one. The unspoken inference being that our demise is somehow an absurdity too ridiculous to imagine. Many are unaware that Ecclesiastes eloquently sums up the matter so much more appropriately with, "...all is vanity."[94]

Perhaps a dramatic close would be to reveal that this writer is weeks, nay even days away from his own demise. And this would then be the adieu to civilization before passing. Neat phrase that, 'passing', wouldn't you say? Yet not only is it true, and therefore misleading and manipulative, but the reality is nonetheless uncomfortably, dare the phrase be suggested in this context, 'imminent.' Yes, true, not only for the writer, but also for those reading this modest effort and even those multitudes that shall never darken these pages with their shadows.

Endings often beg many questions, which may never be answered. Bigger endings, presumably then evolve larger issues that then demand answers of greater magnitude that may also not ever be found in the human realm.

The missionary that suggested God would not cut short His work while she was in the midst of hers is remembered. And certainly, God, were He to deign the time ripe for the inspiring of the ushering in of one final great warning, would choose someone of the stature of the men of God of old, someone of the significance of...well, may we believe the words of Y'shua? "Assuredly I say to you, among those born of women there has not risen one greater than John the Baptist, but he who is least in the kingdom of heaven is greater than he." (Matt. 11:11[95])

Mr. Shakespeare acknowledged then, even so, parting is not always such sweet sorrow. Sometimes it is joy unspeakable and full of Glory!

And so in closing, though much more needs to be considered, and too small furrows have been traced in such a large and foreboding field, this writer finishes in the understanding that for any more additional thoughts, *now has become too late*.

"...Thy Kingdom Come..."[96]

Mesquite, Texas
Sept. 13, 2001

Revised
Sept. 28, 2004

Endnotes

Prologue:
1. Pg. xi - *Matthew* 24:35, the Apostle Matthew, circa A.D. 65.

Chapter I:
2. Pg. 13 - *Chicago Tribune*, March 21, A.D. 2001.
3. Pg. 14 - *Every Prophecy of the Bible*, pg. 10, Walvoord, John F., Chariot Victor Publishing, A.D. 1998. Dr. Walvoord went to be with the Lord December 2001.
4. Pg. 15 - *The Baptist Standard*, pgs. 1 & 12, Dallas, TX, June 25, A.D. 2001.
5. Pg. 15 - *Ibid*. pg. 5, *Down Home* editorial, Knox, Marv, July 30, A.D. 2001.
6. Pg. 16 - *Ecclesiastes*, 1:13, King Solomon, circa B.C. 970.
7. Pg. 17 - *The Genesis Factor*, Rambsel, Yacov, pgs. 161 & 164, Lion's Head Publishing, Beverly Hills, CA, A.D. 2000.
8. Pg. 18 - *I Thessalonians 4:17*, the Apostle Paul, circa A.D. 51.
9. Pg. 18 - *The Gospel of John* 17:20-21, the Apostle John, circa A.D. 26 to 33.
10. Pg. 18 - *Romans* 10:13, the Apostle Paul, winter ending A.D. 57.
11. Pg. 19 - *Hebrews* 3:7, the Apostle Paul, prior to Temple destruction of A.D. 70, see Heb. 10:11.

Chapter II:
12. Pg. 21 - *The King Is Coming* telecast, World Prophetic Ministries, guest lecturer Dr. Tim LaHaye, spring A.D. 2001. Dr. Ed Hindson replaced Dr. Breese, who went to be with the Lord in May 2001.
13. Pg. 22 - *Revelation* 1:7, the Apostle John, circa A.D. 96.

14. Pg. 22 - *I Thess. 4:13.*
15. Pg. 22 - *Rom. 12:15.*
16. Pg. 22 - *John 11:36.*
17. Pg. 22 - *Heb. 9:27.*
18. Pg. 23 - *Matt. 24:29.*
19. Pg. 23 - *Luke 21:36*, the Apostle Luke, the beloved physician, A.D. 60's.
20. Pg. 23 - *Rev. 3:10.*
21. Pg. 23 - *I Thess. 5:8.*
22. Pg. 23 - *I Thess. 4:14.*
23. Pg. 24 - *I Corinthians 15:52*, the Apostle Paul, circa A.D. 59.

Chapter III:
24. Pg. 25 - *WWW.jvim.com.*
25. Pg. 25 - *"Measuring Time With Light"*, Amanda Onion, http://abcnews.go.com, July 12, A.D. 2001.
26. Pg. 26 - *John 8:12.*
27. Pg. 26 - *I Cor. 15:52.*
28. Pg. 26 - *Heb. 9:27.*
29. Pg. 27 - *The Latin Vulgate*, Jerome, circa A.D. 400.
30. Pg. 27 - *I Cor. 15:55.*
31. Pg. 27 - *Hosea 13:14*, the Prophet Hosea, B.C. 785.
32. Pg. 27 - *I Cor. 15:49.*
33. Pg. 27 - *I John 3:2*, the Apostle John, circa A.D. 90.
34. Pg. 27 - *Numbers 10:2*, Moses, circa B.C. 1550.
35. Pg. 28 - *Isaiah 26:3*, the Prophet Isaiah, circa B.C. 712, KJV 1974.

Chapter IV:
36. Pg. 29 - *Heb. 9:28.*
37. Pg. 30 - *John 14:6.*
38. Pg. 30 - *Matt. 25:13.*
39. Pg. 30 - *Rev. 19:10.*
40. Pg. 30 - *I Thess. 5:6,9 & 11.*
41. Pg. 31 - *I Thess. 4:18 & 5:11.*
42. Pg. 31 - *Is. 13:6-10*, circa B.C. 712.
43. Pg. 32 - *I Thess. 4:18.*

44. Pg. 32 - *I Thess. 5:1-3*.
45. Pg. 33 - See works of: Dr. David Breese, Dr. Ed Hindson, Dave Hunt, Hal Lindsey & Dr. Jack Van Impe.
46. Pg. 33 - *I Thess. 5:3c*.
47. Pg. 33 - *Luke 31:36*.
48. Pg. 33 - *Every Prophecy of the Bible*, Scripture Index: pg. 680.
49. Pg. 34 - *Luke 21:25-28*.
50. Pg. 34 - *Rev. 4:1*.
51. Pg. 34 - *Num. 10:7*.
52. Pg. 34 - *Acts 4:38*, Luke, circa A.D. 33.

Chapter V:

53. Pg. 37 - *Coral Ridge newsletter*, Dr. D. James Kennedy, June 11, A.D. 2001.
54. Pg. 37 - *www.coralridge.org*.
55. Pg. 38 - *Operation Save America*, www.operationsaveamerica.org., Flip Benham, Director.
56. Pg. 38 - *Mark 16:16*, the Apostle John Mark, A.D. 26.
57. Pg. 38 - *CRM*.
58. Pg. 38 - *Concerned Women of America*, www.cwfa.org.
59. Pg. 40 - *Twister*, released October 1, 1996.
60. Pg. 41 - *Rom. 10:13*, NKJV.
61. Pg. 41 - *Luke 18:13-14*.

Chapter VI:

62. Pg. 44 - *I Cor. 13:8*.
63. Pg. 44 - *Job 7:6*, suggested author Moses, time period of Job B.C. 1520, written circa B.C. 1491 to 1451.
64. Pg. 45 - *Jesus, The Great Debate*, Jeffrey, Dr. Grant R., Frontier Research Publications, A.D. 1999.
65. Pg. 48 - *II Corinthians 6:16-17*, The Apostle Paul, circa A .D. 60.

Chapter VII:

66. Pg. 55 - *The Late Great Planet Earth*, Lindsey, Hal, May, A.D. 1970.
67. Pg. 56 - *I John 5:13*.

68. Pg. 59 - 20/20, ABC, Barbara Walters/Jane Fonda Interview, spring A.D. 2001.
69. Pg. 60 - www.thekingiscoming.com

Chapter VIII:
70. Pg. 60 - *Matt. 10:32-33.*
71. Pg. 61 - *Matt. 6:34, KJV, 1974.*
72. Pg. 61 - *Heb. 3:13, & 10:25.*
73. Pg. 63 - *Rev. 6:10.*
74. Pg. 63 - *Job 7:6.*
75. Pg. 63 - *II Peter 3:3*, the Apostle Peter, A.D. 66.

Chapter IX:
76. Pg. 65 - *Rom. 9:28.*
77. Pg. 67 - *Is. 53:7.*
78. Pg. 68 - *Eph. 1:4.*
79. Pg. 69 - *Acts 1:6c*, A.D. 33.
80. Pg. 69 - *Matt. 16:18.*
81. Pg. 69 - *I Thess. 4:17a.*

Chapter X:
82. Pg. 71 - *Dr. McGee went to be with the Lord, the morning of Dec. 1, 1988.*
83. Pg. 72 - *Revelation, a Commentary*, McGee, Dr. J. Vernon; Introduction, pg. 9, A.D. 1979.

Chapter XI:
84. Pg. 77 - *II Pet. 3:4.*
85. Pg. 78 - *II Pet. 3:14.*

Epilogue:
86. Pg. 79 - *Rev. 22:6.*
87. Pg. 80 - *John 4:35.*
88. Pg. 80 - *Matt. 13:39.*
89. Pg. 81 - *Galatians 5:11*, the Apostle Paul, A.D. 58.
90. Pg. 81 - *Gal. 6:10.*
91. Pg. 81 - *Luke 11:2, NKJV.*

92. Pg. 81 - *Matt. 24:35*.
93. Pg. 82 - *Ephesians 1:10*, the Apostle Paul, A.D. 61.
94. Pg. 82 - *Eccl. 1:2*.
95. Pg. 83 - *Matt. 11:11*.
96. Pg. 83 - *Matt. 6:10*.

Printed in the United States
129376LV00003B/31/A